Dancing with Spirit, Rooted in Light

Conversations & Inspiration
from the Holy Spirit

Julie M. Krakora

Dancing with Spirit, Rooted in Light:
Conversations & Inspiration from the Holy Spirit
© 2020 Julie M. Krakora

As a piece of personal prayer, every attempt has been made to
make entities mentioned in journal entries anonymous.

Cover image "Encounter" by Mary Southard, CSJ
*Used with permission. Mary Southard retains sole ownership and rights
to this image.* Visit her work at: www.marysouthardart.org

First Edition
1st Printing, November 2020
Printed in the United States of America

Paperback ISBN 978-1-09834-132-9

Christian Spirituality/Prayer Life/ Devotional/Catholic Author

For "the One who loves me the most"
and whom my soul longs to see face to face

Table of Contents

Introduction   pg. 9

How to read "Julie"   pg. 12

Chapter 1: Seeking to Know God
Speak to Me	pg. 16
Stir my Heart	pg. 18
Complete Holiness	pg. 20
Be	pg. 22
Living Prayer	pg. 25
Wrestling with Presence	pg. 27
spirit seeking Spirit	pg. 29

Chapter 2: Seeking Stillness in Prayer
Beauty in Stillness	pg. 32
Be Still	pg. 34
The Way of the Child	pg. 36
Sent to be Prayer	pg. 39
Bring God Home	pg. 41
Rooted Love	pg. 43
Vessel of Peace	pg. 46

Chapter 3: Peering into God's Heart
Presence Shines	pg. 50
The Womb of God	pg. 53
In the Center	pg. 56
Integrated Soul	pg. 58
Etched into Light	pg. 61
Buried in Holiness	pg. 64
Faith of a Child	pg. 66

Chapter 4: Learning from Nature

Chasing the Sun	pg. 70
Sound of Prayer	pg. 73
Surrender into Serenity	pg. 75
Posture of Prayer *(when dust sparks life)*	pg. 78
Fluid Motion	pg. 81
Prayer In and Out of Creation	pg. 84
Blossom Benevolence	pg. 86

Chapter 5: Leaning into Trust

Beyond Illusions to Grace	pg. 90
Enter into Presence	pg. 92
Reverent Joy	pg. 95
Punctuated Prayer	pg. 98
Strength of the Summons	pg. 101
Tandem Dance	pg. 104
"Dear World"	pg. 106

Chapter 6: Choosing to Gift Praise

A Soultender's Prayer	pg. 110
Candlemas Prayer	pg. 113
Precipice Prayer	pg. 115
In Service of Triduum	pg. 117
Soul Breaths	pg. 120
Fallow Ground of Grace	pg. 123
Soul Providers	pg. 125

Chapter 7: Singing Soulfully

Grandeur of God	pg. 128
Wrap your Soul in Song	pg. 130
Spirit Dances	pg. 133
Dancing with Spirit, Rooted in Light	pg. 137
Secured Soulfulness	pg. 139
Fashioned Praise	pg. 141
Life-Song Seeker	pg. 143

Chapter 8: Plunging into Mercy

Instructions of Grace	pg. 148
Cultivating God's Breath	pg. 150
Evidence of Breath	pg. 153
Divine Mercy Sunday	pg. 155
Fire & Ocean of Mercy	pg. 159
Vineyard of Heart	pg. 162
Unspoken Strength	pg. 164

Encounter – Closing Thoughts

Encounter – Closing Thoughts	pg. 169
Acknowledgements	pg. 172

Acknowledgements

If You spoke to me in riddles
it would be easier to say I cannot comprehend.

But You speak to me so clearly
that my heart must hear, abide by Your will,
and follow this clear, yet invisible plan.

I am held, loved, given interior gifts
and know not the final outcome.

Yet presence seems to be enough at times,
to quietly minister and change ways,
while the mind still longs
to understand the process.

Can You enlighten me a bit more?
I already seek You constantly
and thrive in Your world and not the other.

Grant me peace to deal with me.

February 3, 2011

INTRODUCTION

My family and closest friends know that I am a reflective person who lives for God and connects easily to Him. I have spent my life heavily involved in the Catholic Church, both personally and professionally. Being in a Catholic Church was like an indoor spiritual playground, a second home. As a five-year-old, Sisters at our parish joked I would become Sr. Julie. (I never heard that call within me.) Fast-forward years later to my sophomore year in high school when our youth minister confidently declared I would be the first Roman Catholic female priest, (obviously not a possibility in our time.) Though I was quiet and insecure about every area in my life, I was the opposite when it came to my faith.

As noted above, my faith is tangible to others and throughout my life I've been aware of strangers gazing at me with odd, yet kind, looks. This often happens just after I've been to Mass or have been immersed in prayer. I assume they sense the Holy Spirit still strongly dwelling within me, but they don't quite know what to make of it. I usually just smile back and go upon my merry way. But certain comments stay with you a long time, and one such comment rekindled the fire to publish this book.

In the fall of 2016, I was invited to be the speaker at a Women's Advent Retreat for my home parish. Though a few women on the planning committee knew me, many did not, so I came to a meeting to introduce myself and hear their thoughts about what they wanted to accomplish for the retreat. Then I shared my intentions for my presentation through what God had told me earlier in the week. I explained that I have "date times" with Him in a nearby nature preserve and tend to write down the experience and what He speaks, or places on my heart, in my journal. That particular day God spoke so quickly that I had to use my phone to record it. I shared the message with the group, thinking nothing of it. At the end of the meeting one of the women looked at me sincerely and said, "I want to go on a God walk with you! Can you teach me how to do what you do?" I was deeply touched by her request yet felt that I could not teach what I was never taught! How could I teach something that has been an innate part of me since childhood?

I never forgot her comment because it was the first time a stranger, who was older than me, saw the gift of my soul and wanted it for her own life. I didn't know how to teach it but hoped to find a way. Mother Mary pondered/reflected on "all these things" (Luke 2:19, 2:51) about Jesus – His true identity noted by the angels and prophets, and His knowledge teaching in the temple as a boy – and kept them in her heart. She was aware of His mission. Like her I tucked away the inner understanding of an additional mission, to offer my insights, into my heart and quietly pondered it for years. And ever since then, I have been more conscious of close friends and acquaintances affirming and pushing me to share and teach what defines who I am.

In truth, I have been doing this professionally for years. I have worked with junior high and high school youth and their parents, as well as college students and faculty. It seems that no matter my role or the ages I work with, I am always teaching about the need for prayer. I'm not talking about the obligatory prayers made before meals and asking for healing for friends and family. Of course, those are beneficial, but they fall short of a grander opportunity. The type of prayer I encourage is one that fosters a relationship with our Creator, based upon a supposition of a shared desire to spend time with one another. The kind where you and God both share your innermost thoughts and feelings, just as you would with a best friend. And, just as the process of gaining a best friend takes time, dedication, and good will toward one another, the same is true of becoming best friends with the Almighty.

I have always felt my purpose in life is to help people find God and establish a deep, loving relationship with Him. I personally don't know how I could exist without His love and our frequent conversations. This book is a just a drop in the ocean of many writings recording our conversations. Most of the writings are His responses to my questions and struggles on any given day; while others are expressions of gratitude, love, or curiosity on my part. My sincere desire is that by sharing these with you, your soul will be stirred to take your own relationship with God to new, deeper, and higher levels.

May you be blessed in your time to hear God speak to you differently through the vessel of my prayer time with Him. I pray you are touched and transformed to grow deeper into God's beloved heart.
~ Julie M. Krakora ~

HOW TO READ "JULIE"

This is how a friend of mine refers to reading my work, and she wished to share some suggestions for getting the most out of each poem, based upon her few years of experience.

- These are not "quick reads," so don't try to read more than one per day.

- Find a quiet space, take a few deep breaths, and open your mind.

- Because Julie's writings are so personal, the entire entry may be overwhelming. Read slowly and take time to re-read.

- Julie writes from her heart, but most of the prayers and insights are universal.

- Enjoy the beautiful flow of her words, then contemplate what it means for you.

- Make sure you give yourself time to use her questions and reflections to allow yourself to go deeper. Write your answers and insights down in order to practice giving voice to your own connection with God.

Before you begin reading the fruit of prayer in my life, I invite you to take a brief spiritual inventory of your relationship with God. Whatever your answers to the questions below, you are encouraged to look at them throughout your journey as a reminder of any promise you choose to make between yourself and God at this time. Hopefully when you finish reading, you will see the fruit of prayer in a stronger, ever evolving, relationship with Him.

- **Where and when do you currently feel most connected to God's love and feel His presence?**

- **At what times do you feel the least connected?**

- **What changes in your relationship would you like to see?**

- **What habits are you willing to start to invite God in your daily life?**

Now, are you ready to dance with the Holy Spirit? To be more rooted in the light God wants you to claim? Each chapter offers thematic questions so you can choose a topic that fits for your day. Or you can read each chapter (slowly and prayerfully) in order (or not!) Any prayer response heard directly from God will always be *in italicized print.*

Finally, under the "Personal Focus" section you will usually find some background of what led me to the prayer writing from my voice or God's response. Each entry also gives a few questions to reflect on quietly, or if you are willing, to journal. Allow God's Spirit, who touches me so constantly, find and guide you!

Chapter 1
Seeking to Know God

*Have you ever struggled to accept the holiness God graces us,
by virtue of our baptism, in being His beloved daughter or son?*

*Truthfully, hidden deep inside us, I think we all struggle
with feeling like we are enough for those we love.*

*That inner voice which speaks and questions,
then lifts towards God wondering the same thing.*

*How can I allow myself to be loved by
immense pure beautiful Light who is Love?*

Speak to me

Spirit of Truth, present in my soul,
speak to me the words I need to hear
Statements of belief to affirm my path,
and breathe life into a willing and entrusted temple
who desires to be pure and true.

If I am yours and You are mine,
may grace and energy continue to flow
with acknowledgement of the lessons that
float by on our stream of conscious thought.

You are near and multiplied in many forms on this planet
under names that desperately seek to fashion an identity
for an entity that contains all of us
without rules and disciplines.

Here we are ~ holding hearts in open arms
to offer thanksgiving to our God
who is above us,
within us,
all around us.
May the mercy and
peace our hearts and our world need
come to fruition.
Amen.

August 8, 2006

Personal Focus

Entry prior to that message said: "I want to write – not sure where to start and even if I should start writing my truth. I've always felt that something needs to be shared. Spirit God guide me to know the gifts You desire I use in this world. Help me accept, love, and see the goodness that is me all the time. May I know and find peace within."

- **What gifts has God given you in all realms of your being: physical, emotional, intellectual, spiritual?**

- **How can you trust God more to help you use these gifts today? And what doubts hold you back from feeling like God is present to you today and every day to come?**

- **What hopes do you hold for the world?**

Stir my Heart

Oh presence of God within me,
draw out that which deadens my senses.
Light the fire to stir my heart to action.
May my ponderings become certainties
and fears flying aimlessly be put to rest.

Searching only to *be* who I *already* am and
to heal that which is saddened within me.
Angels are present to take my hand -
to dance and laugh,
to gently sing and praise, and
to lovingly comfort and hold me.

All in One
You choose to become real in each of us.
resurrecting the life You desired
from the beginning of time.

Open our hearts and minds to all in our path,
all which leads us closer to the fullness of Light
and calls us home.

December 12, 2006

Personal Focus

I wrote this while on a retreat with juniors at the high school connected to my work parish. I was pondering my presence to a certain student who was struggling and also a young adult colleague. While I helped them, I still struggled to know my true purpose.

- **When people come to you for help, how do you respond? In your response, do you see God working in you? Can you discern God's plan from the situations that cross your path?**

- **What is your understanding of, or relationship with, your guardian angel(s)? Do you actively ask for their help in your path and for others you love?**

Complete Holiness

The places you create in your heart
are masterpieces to be found and uncovered.
You seek the world,
its hidden treasures and obscured answers,
without fully understanding your heart.
You seek truth and justice
without first practicing its essence in your reality.

This dichotomy of living confuses you,
holds you captive to the old
while longing deeply for the new.

Sit with your holiness.
Discover the treasure of your heart.
Only then can you give it away
in service, in love, and
in complete holiness for all of creation.

You, child, are gift.
Recognize your light
and let it shine in abundance for many to see.

Be unafraid of what blessings you call forth-
they are gold to the energetic nature of the world.
Recall - child of love, of hope, of pure heart-
that you affect change by living it out
and believing in the great essence of love.

As you seek less glory for yourself
and more wholeness for those in your path,
you affect the change your heart longs to see.

April 23, 2007

Personal Focus

I started my entry with this quote from the book I was reading: *"Compassionate self-awareness leads to change; harsh self-criticism only holds the patterns in place creating a stubborn and defensive basic self. Be gentle with yourself as you would with a child. Be gentle but firm. Give yourself the space to grow. But remember that the timing is in God's hands, NOT yours."* (**Sacred Journey of the Peaceful Warrior** by Dan Millman.) In reflecting on that, and before I heard God's response in my heart, I wrote: "I am too busy for my own good. If I keep up this pace and do not step back, I will forget about me and go backwards. Taking a step forward to be gentle with myself is the direction I need to go."

- **How do you listen to your heart? Do you know, and understand, its desires?**

- **What do you hide from God, though God sees and still loves in you?**

- **In what ways are you afraid of your potential greatness? What caused this? How can you pray through this?**

BE...

Part 1: *You are going inward child to a place you have known in times of past and need to rediscover. You need to simultaneously learn to open, heal, soothe, and protect your heart. There is an urging in your soul to be solidly planted in your own soul and 'forced' to have to follow through to commit and share. We need not speak so strongly when you do what is necessary at the time.*

This is a time or pruning away the old to prepare for the glorious new dawn which has already begun. Oh, child of light, if you could experience that freeness in dance throughout life, and love who you are so completely at all times, things would be easier for you. You are still so humble and shy for you [yet] in song with teens, with children, you explode into the radiance where your soul longs to reside.

Have you not figured out that you are not, cannot, remain in the dark? You do know this, and your place of work does not prevent this from occurring.

Live your calling. Accept your heart. Be at peace with what you create. Your spirit knew it needed a rest and a healthier cocooning time. While you dislike the stillness/aloneness on your hands, you are doing well. Believe in yourself. You have the answers you seek.

Part 2:
Trust the fullness within your hearts
that grows in exceeding passion to create more life.
There is much need to reside within the stillness
of your hearts and minds these days.
As the earth sleeps in her blanket of snow
and settles the roots of waiting flowers,
you do the same.

Without proper time
to get outside of the chaos of everyday life,
you lose sight of the precious moments
of existence you can create.
It is impossible to move forward without rest,
without recharging your external batteries
with the One who created your Light.
Some of you already see this need
and have fulfilled your soul's desires.

Be creative in your growth.
Trust what occurs before you
allow each opportunity to feed the depth of your being.
Dance.
Accept life.
Accept peace.
Treasure the love you already have and...
in gratitude pass this glorious gift to others.

Be.
Tenderly love yourself and your lives.
Allow yourself time to be nurtured.
Just be.

Be Light. Be radiance.
Be joy. Be you.
Just be.

February 1, 2008

Personal Focus

Prior to hearing God speak to me in that response to my heart, I wrote of being quiet, yet anxious in an unspoken way. I felt a great shift occurring within me. I am incredibly cautious about who I trust with my spiritual journey but was compelled to meet Alice, a spiritual director my friend spoke of highly. I called Alice the evening of this entry and think I was anxious but excited. Looking back, Alice become a massive gift for the 5 years we met. She helped me "be" and offer a safe space to be real and more spiritual growth came from this trusting space.

- **Do you struggle to fully trust others? If you have difficulty in this, do you know why?**

- **Who do you allow to journey with, guide, or even direct your spiritual life?**

- **What demands your attention so you feel you cannot spend time peacefully in prayer?**

- **How can you choose to craft more time to worship God and to honor the vessel of life He created you to be, thus living and "just being" in that moment?**

Living Prayer

You are prayer in how you live your life,
in the moments you breathe in the splendor of creation
As you observe the masterpiece unfold and partake in its beauty
you hold the world in grace
  in that tiny moment of thanks.

You wonder how to pray and what to pray?
Is it not the calling of your life to be prayer walking?
To unfurl the harshness back into the atmosphere
by bringing a body of peace into contact with danger?

As you live is as you are
Do not forget to honor who you are
to be this being of light at all times
even when you forget,
  the light still shines, explosively!

Don't try to turn down the light, it is meant to shine
Praise the wonders around you
Listen to your heart sing and your soul speak
Marvels are to be found in those sounds
for you hear the voice of God
  in the whispers of stillness
  and in the shouts of praise.

Be blessed on this journey
Think not less of yourself or others
for not speaking prayer at all times
But choose to LIVE prayer, your life, at all times!
Be in accordance with the measure of grace in your soul
Those steps are holy
Your dance is song and will lead you home into glory

March 13, 2008

Personal Focus

I wrote about being excited to be healthy again (I get sick a lot), praying for a friend, and doing a surprise visit to a colleague who needed to be uplifted.

- **How are you open to allowing God to use everything you do to serve Him? What kind of things can you name right now that, with intention, can be better seen or used as prayer?**

- **Do you see your everyday actions as prayer? Why or why not?**

Wrestling with Presence

If You are all that is within me, why do I wonder?
Why does my heart soar to heights unfathomable
to rest in Your presence, yet grow in dis-ease
of the creation of earth (or rather other people?)
I seek You constantly,
long deeply to be held and be of service, simultaneously.
You are not hidden, my God,
You are existing in every place I seek.
The deepest crevice of my being calls out to You.
Resistance of mind and will stifle decisions.
What one part of me innately knows
the other wrestles with, unconsciously,
to claim the truth in time.

Who knew the physical limitations of a body
dancing to be set free
would be such a hindrance?
The spirit of me and the Spirit You are
coexist in a place of pureness.
May this knowledge wash over me,
remind me when I am weak.
It is impossible to thrive here
without Your complete Presence.
Stay near.
Speak clearly.
Respond in a manner that Your voice
may be heard and accepted in my heart and soul.
In my life.

November 4, 2010

Personal Focus

My prayer was the entry for the day. What led to it was found in my journal entry the prior day and spoke of extremely jarring news that a person who did tremendous damage to my psyche and being was about to be back in my lifepath. I know that rocked my world and took its toll in my mind and physically in my body.

- **What are you wrestling with, yet unable to give to God for a reason known only to you? Why are you unwilling to release it?**

- **What holds you back from believing all God says He is for your life?**

spirit seeking Spirit

Dearest God, Beloved Jesus, Sustaining Spirit,
Should I hold You captive in my gaze, will You speak to me forever in a language pure enough for my soul to hear and clear enough for my mind to know? In the nuances of spiral living, there is a journey into You deeper and deeper - moments of expectant and blissful joy and times of uncertain shadows deepening a desire to grow.

Secured into the playful depth of exceeding grace, my being is stretched, poured out, and many times remolded in the fire of Your watchful love. How can this occur over and over again? What is it in me that so resolutely requires the reception into Your being so fully that all decisions, all love, all free-flowing and experienced compassion in me is because of You – not the concrete rules of mankind teaching me what to believe, but the innate knowledge of gifted grace flowering in my soul? You speak to me in reverent and unfolding beauty to capture me, hold me still, touch an area of life in me activated by You alone to know how to live and move, to take part in this world.

How I know You, feel You, and experience Your captivating love does not seem common, but it is not unknown, simply under accepted. Because of this I wonder, yet in moments of doubt neither can I wander. You are life and breath and home to me. I wish to understand all that cannot be understood, for You are the Maker, Lover, Creator of all. Through my desire and also utter ineptness to know Your plan, may I at least be able to choose to live Your will within my steps, choices, and relationships.
With undoubting love, Julie
October 15, 2012

Personal Focus

The entry shared my complete journal entry for the day. I was writing to God how I felt about Him and my needs.

- As the entry is my apparent letter of love to God, if you were to write a love letter to God what would it say? Try and write this letter today (handwritten or a computer document!)

- Aside from daily supplications and petitions for those in need, and for your own needs, how often do you praise God for who He is? Can you add this to your letter? Gratitude is always a gift to hear.

Chapter 2
Seeking Stillness in Prayer

True stillness is elusive.

*For, while we say we want quiet in our life,
it seems we are equally afraid of it.*

How would you qualify your efforts to seek stillness?

*What holds you back from diving inside your soul
and inviting God into the mess of your life?*

Beauty of Stillness

In a manner of speaking, you are satisfied in your core.
But have you truly attained that which you are looking for?
In moments of bliss
angels stand at your side
hold you in glory
laughing as you cry in joy!

Do you not yet know how close they are?
That each moment of breath is a gift?
Speak soundly to your heart
understand its worth
its pleasure
its mission to change the world.

Oh, children of light in this world
if you could only see
beyond the veil you hide behind so gloriously.

Listen. Spend time being still.
Wrap yourselves in cloaks of beauty
and times of silence.
The world is too loud.
The gentlest touch of human compassion
becomes a calming symphony to the world.
Write the masterpiece of melody
uniquely your song
and boldly proclaim it
to all who can hear.

August 19, 2007

Personal Focus

My previous entry was the day before and spoke about seeking direction for the meditation CD I felt called to create. But also, that I was feeling alone and disconnected even though I wrote of five people who were part of the day that touched me.

- **What you are you seeking/needing today?**

- **What veils do you hide behind, not wanting God to see a fear, a failure, or even your true hopes and dreams?**

- **What calling do you have to proclaim the "song of your life?"**

Be Still

Speak no more
of the silent stillness covering the earth.
For in these pure moments of vibrant sound,
that of spectacular nothingness,
everything can be heard
and felt at great lengths.

The notion of sleep heals the mind,
restores the body,
calms the heart.
But if you can bask in the stillness of a night's breath
you grasp onto the radiant goodness
pulsing from light into resonant darkness.

You need not know why the dark exists.
Hold on to the shining moments
of gold in your heart, your life,
for it is here when you tap into your soul.
Share your truth
and touch another's soul.
The silence provides the avenue
to reach the gold of your life.
Mine this often as stillness feeds your soul
and nothingness can quench the fires burning in your heart.

Be still.
Be still and know that I AM your God.
Come and sit with Me awhile.
Spread this goodness and
unwrap the glory of your soul.
You are needed for others.
Exist in this glory to share light and love.

December 2, 2008

Personal Focus

Those words were the entry for the day. Given the previous entry 2 days prior, I had been "frazzled, frustrated, angry and tired" and even time at Mass was difficult. My back went out during Mass and I struggled with that. In my discomfort during the whole Mass, I still found a way to pray. I wrote "I felt rooted in the earth and connected to the heavens simultaneously during the Eucharistic prayer yet struggle with the intensity of what happens to my body when I am in moments of deeper prayer."

- **What is the "gold" of your life, the treasure that makes you "you" and needs to be rediscovered in stillness so God can affirm you?**

- **Are you open or resistant to the idea that you are worthy of God's love? What helped you accept this worthiness or what hinders you from accepting this?**

- **What does "being still" mean to you?**

The Way of the Child

The little child shall lead the wise
into the ways of goodness and truth.
There is no temperament of a soul greater than
the pureness of strength and fragility that a child does possess.
For while incredibly weak
and depending on an adult to care for all needs
he knows more in pure solitude of stillness
from his mother's womb
than any adult in this lifetime.

The earmuffs for the soul are fuzzy and warm.
The blinders bright and cheerful.
This costume of the soul protects the ignorance of those sleeping
until the light of an angel, in the guise of a child,
reminds the player about the greater rules of heaven.

Be still. Be precious. Be loved.
Know I AM your God.
The light seeping through these vessels
protrudes into blocked avenues and for a time, or more,
will heal the tissues, scarred and hidden within.

In the complexity of this world,
it is the grace of little moments which breaks the sound barrier
and allows the soul to sing in glory.
I AM both the child reaching and calling out for protection
and the adult giving love and comfort. Know this.
Treasure this dichotomy of life-giving sustenance
that never ceases to exist.

If I AM in all, I cannot be destroyed.
The light is powerful
and conquers the incomprehensible sadness of the world.
Should you choose to live as this light and to recognize these
moments,
the earth shall return to her full glory.

January 18, 2009

Personal Focus

The theme of my writing included messages about a child needing his father. A St. Jude commercial stirred me. My inner being felt like a child held by God's hands, but the image was that God was both Father and Son simultaneously. And then at my 2nd Mass of the weekend, the priest opened his homily with a story of him unexpectedly holding an 11-month old boy who needed safety and stillness from a tense situation. He shared of how this child taught him.

-   **Are you in touch with your inner child? If so, what is it speaking to you? What might it need?**

-   **What did you love to do as a child?**

-   **Can you remember a moment of pure joy and see how God found and taught you in that joy?**

<u>Sent to be Prayer</u>

I have sent you to be amidst the angst of the world~
to live and breathe fully the existence
of the average and ordinary
while simultaneously calling you
to be extraordinary in your response

You have been questioning Me in this silent time~
not so much My presence, My voice, My direction
but why the silence.
It is to see you solidly grow and be upon your own,
supported in your chosen environment.
You have done well

I have seen you smile in excitement
Felt the tears of your compassion
Known the joy of your heart
You come home to yourself, to Me, in many ways

This is prayer
Prayer of word, of actions
Prayer of silence and song
Prayer of stillness and frustration

You are learning and accepting
that grace appears in many ways
Continue to be thankful
and allow your heart to be open
to share a message of hope and love with an expanding world.

February 14, 2009

Personal Focus

My entry spoke of the gift of two people who had been great companions who helped me grow. I also expressed great frustration from events in life. (Ironically, I tend not to write when I am very stressed, so I referenced 'intensity of Jan 25 – Feb 10'.) I then wrote: "struggling with wanting to be me, to be free in sharing spiritual gifts but conscious of walls stopping me" and the prayer entry happened after that.

- **What in life makes it difficult for you to pray or believe that prayer even works?**

- **When God is silent and seemingly not answering your requests, do you still have patience and believe?**

- **Do you ever ask your Creator to reveal things about yourself to you? What do you need to hear today?**

Bring God Home

Gentle, be gentle with yourself in a time
of great transition and peace needed for yourself.
Within you holds and lives the glory of My heart,
fully abundant and overflowing as you choose to be a vessel.
You hear my voice in the little moments.
You seek My face in the anguished.
You lift your soul to support another.

The work is great child, the laborers plentiful, yet few.
Few because far too many choose to ignore their hearts,
their calling to affect more change.
You need to live out My life purpose, My love for all
in the actions you choose.

Stop questioning. Trust!
Live fully the moments placed before you.
There is strength in suffering and in new birth.
The fight for life, for wholeness, for peace within
was conquered long ago –
but the message was lost.

If you have eyes to see,
see the truth.
If you have a voice,
use it to proclaim the goodness you know and experience.

Most abundantly and importantly…
LIVE that which is set before you.
Choose to then change this world and bring Me home.

March 23, 2009

Personal Focus

Words prior to the message: "Once I think I know what I'm doing, I don't!" Always, so true. I was getting frustrated at my inability to balance work (need to stay late) with my non-work parish's choir practice with a new choir director. Working with youth, their struggles are carried in me. An 8th grade boy was struggling to believe in God and thus conflicted about his choice to be Confirmed in a month. Yet, in all this, a catechist/friend shared what I had done to make a difference.

- **What makes you overwhelmed? And, in that sense of being overwhelmed, how do you invite God into your mess?**

- **In what ways are you a laborer doing God's will?**

- **How often have you pondered your purpose in life? What questions do you have for God about your place and time here on earth?**

Rooted Love

In stillness you stand beating a heartbeat for two
not realizing the effect of your placement in this world
to see the world with eyes of others,
to feel the passion bursting in frozen walls,
to know the innate beauty resting in soft moments.

You are called to exist in the now,
to claim your heart, held in Mine,
and then draw into this one Love the hearts of others.

Bigger than laws which confound your spirit,
the grace in your soul roots you
to explore and change the pattern,
ever mindful to hold the promise
of beauty from which it began.

The task is as simply complex
as the passionate prayer of transformation
you already know exists
within those painful moments of goodbye.

In the now, honor the past.
Be at peace with challenged responses
and allow the future to unfold in harmonious grace.

I require none other than this from you:
to remain rooted in My love
and to speak passionately
that which we experience together
in a union all desire to feel and yet feel unworthy to accept.
You thrive here.

You need the complexity of simplistic union to survive.
When all start living in Oneness,
the energy of this world can change.
Hold fast child.
Remain steadfast in this deep-rooted love.

October 27, 2009

Personal Focus

What preceded this prayer time was quite complicated and painful. Having Celiac disease, it means I cannot receive the host, the Body of Christ, and at the time could only receive from the Cup, the Precious Blood. My parish suddenly chose to take the Cup away out of fear of illness. I spoke up and was incredibly ill-received, and thus emotionally hurt by a few people on staff there. I wrote: "I need the physical meal to ground me within the community I have loved. Without that 'thread', both being Eucharist and choir (which I had then stepped away from) it is too easy to lose my connection to this parish which has been utterly amazing. I've had the best (in terms of a tremendous spiritually filling Mass) and cannot accept anything less. But are You calling me to a change? To suffer for others as my mom suggests? Or call forth more passion and compassion from me? What have You required of me?"

- Even when life is painful, God still seeks something from us. What do you think that is for you?

- What, or who, is your community that helps you thrive?

- What moments feed your soul, allowing you to thrive? Do you recognize God in those moments?

- How is what you are doing, or the role you are playing in life, bringing God into the world?

<u>Vessel of Peace</u>

Flowing though the vessel of sustained healing
she cries for massive change and shakes
in acknowledgement of the ability to proceed.

In essence, her rumbling
is the clarion wake-up call to seek within,
unearth the powerful peace needed,
to protect each person from the chaos of a fighting world.

The passion to resist is not necessary.
The strength to recognize and retain goodness
creates the detachment to see beyond now.

If peace is stirring in your soul
let it flow, unhindered, into muddled surroundings.
One life of precious presence sustains manifold.
Claim the truth of the life force flowing effortlessly within.

Share the richness of this nectar
with those who desire to taste the goodness.
Be the beacon brilliantly burning.
Engage the heart in creative dance
to learn a new beat
to walk a golden path.

The vessel contained within a masterpiece of crafted prayer
can change eternity.
The spirit reaches out in hope
in anticipation of the next phase in life
unconscious to the stirrings of planetary wisdom.

February 10, 2010

Personal Focus

My explanation came after what I heard from God. "I felt something coming but didn't expect that! I have been aware since last week that I am more at ease as life has drastically slowed down. [I switched parishes] and have felt the movement of spirit at [new parish] which has been the impetus for pondering this week. In a conversation with a friend there, she shared words that helped me hear my role and place to be present in that community. Her words blessed me for a moment in recognition of the presence I choose to both hold/be and only hope that I can as easily share.

-   **Do you accept that you are the temple of the Holy Spirit – a vessel of God?**

-   **When difficulties, or resistance to what is holy or good, come your way, how do you respond?**

-   **What helps you continue to do your best even when you feel unsupported?**

-   **How do you help our earth to be a better and healthier place to live?**

Chapter 3
Peering into God's Heart

*Your image of God colours your conversation
with God and even how you might choose
to receive comfort and love from God.*

Who is God to you?

What is your image of God?

*If you can see and define your image,
can you be in better relationship with God
and allow God to transform your life,
or at least your struggles in life?*

Presence Shines

You have asked me to sit at your feet
place my hands into yours
and allow this heart to flood into one.
In true presence, united in antiquated and vibrant love,
we exist together *(though this does not feel like enough at times.)*

So, You surprise me as You cause my feet to dance
      tap into the blessings of accepted laughter
      waltz within the compassion of being known
      float into abandon as hearts cry out to each other.
In friendship Your face shines, Your voice is heard,
Your love aptly felt.
I need You – yet I am needed too –
needed to feel and shine Your love.

It takes many, many to somehow
exemplify the expansiveness
of who You truly are in my life.
Why within You I am enough
and without You I endlessly search and lose hope.

You remind me in the promise of presence,
looking into the soul of a friend with unspoken words,
that I am somehow worth it
in this floundering abyss of surface living.

As we climb deeper, the presence changes,
magnifies the giftedness
proclaims the innate beauty shining within.
As I soak in your Presence, alone, and in others
fill this core, treat the woundedness.

Allow me to simply do more to bring forth grace
share the experience of love
shine out the attitude of peace needed in our world.

Only the simplest notion remains through this call,
In your Presence, I am truly home.

October 20, 2009

Personal Focus

I wrote the prior day: "I need to remain wholly connected to the greatness and sweetness of You to survive in a very tough and lonely culture. I seek guidance for the steps of my heart in expanding my faith and my community." Then the next day I was conscious of, and extremely grateful for, all the moments where I was touched by others or my presence helped them.

-   **How do you express your love to God?**

-   **How do you allow the feelings of your heart to flow out into *the love letter of your life* for God to see and, more importantly, hear?**

-   **What pulls your soul to acknowledge the blessings of life?**

-   **Who are the people that make God come more to life for you?**

The Womb of God

Longing mostly to be held, loved, and nurtured
the unseen stronger spirit, acknowledging
complete weakness,
wanted one thing and one thing only -
to be renewed in the arms of her Creator.

Assumed into the expansiveness of God
prime space for sighing exists in...
letting go
      being fed
            receiving love.

God?
God wisely knows best and transforms
the desires of heart and mind.
Granted the acknowledgement of total surrender to Love,
is this a beginning?
An end?

Expansiveness of unknowing compositions of light
surround a presence so used to form.
I desired the warmth of Creator's lap
I was given the blessing of Creator's womb.

Backward in time
can we be made new
again
and again
and again?

The womb of God offered no answers
simply space
and immensity of God's love
to continue giving and sharing love.
Lost in this sea of fluid comprehension
my identity was stripped
cleansed
returned anew.

If I have truly reentered the womb of God,
how do I live this truth on earth?

May 14, 2010

Personal Focus

This entry is about exploring an image I saw and felt during an acupuncture session. At times I am open to 'energy' and know that when I call upon God to help heal me, things happen. I felt so safe and calm during this session as evidenced in these words: "I wanted so much to just crawl back into the lap of God and something else transpired, 'the womb of God.'" I was literally within God and saw many lights around me. It was heavenly, healing, and brought forth awareness of things I needed to change. From this point forward, my image of God became a "womb"-encompassed, protected, wanted, and loved.

- **Who is God to you?**

- **Deeply reflect, paint in your mind, and feel in your heart and soul, what God "looks like" as a feeling for how you feel loved and known by God. Once you have seen your image, take time to write (or sketch) this down.**

In the Center

In the center of the deepest core of your soul
sits a presence so soft and humble
longing to be acknowledged and held.

The unwounded master key to Our relationship
is not tested, just protected
so as to assure the safe passage of light and love
seeping back into your soul.

Placating the mind works for only so long
Unfettered resistance is broken when silence arrives
seeps into crevices unknown
acts as ointment and oil for your essence
to speak and hear My words.

Winding through the maze of life, longing, and even love,
the center is always the resting point
both in purpose to acknowledge the journey within
and to prepare the heart to reenter the world.

Found, captivated, and made whole
in the center we reunite and dance to lullabies
for a resting child-hearted soul.
The overgrowth of this path need not exist
if you seek the center of life often.

Come then child, find Me, and
explore the heavens and the universe above
while healing and honoring the heavens
woven into your soul

In the center you remember, fortify your being
and receive gifts to offer the world.

June 1, 2010

Personal Focus

The weather was perfect for a walk, code name: 'let's go to the labyrinth to be outside, soak in silence, and pray!' I walked for clarity, wisdom, strength, and the needs of a few friends, specifically one. At the end of my time in the labyrinth and writing the prayer poem, I wrote this. "Tonight, was about letting go, receiving, and resting in the Spirit. I literally felt drugged from the peace. I had been speaking in tongues momentarily while I prayed in the center. Thanks God, for the clarity and opening and fixing my heart."

- **In what situations do you "think" you are trusting and turning to God, but truly still holding tight to your own ways and not allowing God in?**

- **What are your ways to 'go to the center' or your soul to be found by God?**

- **Consider walking a Labyrinth to pray with and untangle your thoughts.** Find one at: *www.labyrinthlocator.com/locate-a-labyrinth*

  Want to know more how to pray with a labyrinth? Try this website: *www.franciscanmedia.org/labyrinths-the-inward-journey*

Integrated Soul

When called into the frenzied stillness of chartered paths
The known is unknown
Words become unreasonable
Sight appears invisible
The paradox of kairos time

Grounded under the magisterium of bellowing,
and swaying green on high
proclaims that only surrender is acceptable.
Is it possible to greet Me, know Me, love Me
in the emptying of your life?

My child, you know this to be true
and the gift of resilient truth you receive
feeds and bathes your hungry soul.
Time stands still.
We greet each other in full reverence, for
not only do you seek to reside nestled into My being,
I desire to remain integrated into your being.

The footsteps into this timeless love are never measured in pace,
simply taken.
You cannot stumble
but you can choose to stop
before ready-ing your soul to receive Me.

There are unique moments of communion
in your knowledge of Eucharist received
among and from people – a most sacred time.
And also, with union to own your chosen path
to acknowledge the uncertain
to crave the completeness found in the center.

Community is vital to grasp My love.
Quietness is essential
to instill this gift into the crevices of your life.
All may choose to come
though many do not.
Once you know of the rich nectar of this profound treasure of love
(stillness in your core)
your path
your choices
the intimate details of your life
are never the same.
In reception of and in union of time held in My arms
You are loved, captured, but also set free.

June 20, 2010

Personal Focus

The prior day was my first time writing in 19 days. I shared that much was going on and I was trying to understand it all. Some had to do with relationships in family and another with trying to understand this seemingly good, yet unusually deep, connection with a friend. I was talking with others and writing emails to friends but hadn't showed up to my prayer journal. Thus, that evening was beautiful and per usual, I walked and found myself at the church's labyrinth. I walked it to process thoughts, bring them to God, and specifically to hear God. God certainly responded to bring peace to a chattering soul that needed to be quiet.

- **When do you choose (or need) to walk into true stillness?**

- **If you don't, what stops you?**

- **When you arrive, do you give yourself time to get rid of the monkey-mind, so the treasure of God's voice is ready to be received?**

Etched into Light

Recognition of beauty in vibrant and sullen leaves
remains a mystery to the seeking soul.
Nuances of light tamper with cells and forge strength and courage
where there is none to be found.
In the creative blending of light and air
the compulsion to grow, fall, live, is etched into living stone.

Taken over by and captured into My grace
you will be, and are, continually transformed.
In death there is purpose,
in life there is both pain and rebirth.

Resurrected moments occur when acceptance is given
over and over again.
Thus the polishing of one's armor is gleaned
to re-gift the world anew,
to charge the soul to a higher vibration,
an ability to listen to My voice,
and to wait in soulful stillness for new people to come.

Processing the means to new life cannot be named,
for it happens uniquely, individually,
with soulful purpose to re-shift thinking
and reclaim an identity gloriously gifted to you at birth.

And when this death occurs,
as you are given over into Light,
for a moment in time,
the blessing you offer is a choice to shine
and color the world with an array of constant blessings.

Through transformative moments,
until an ending birthed to the ground,
your brilliance can still touch the world
as you become My rose petals of love blanketing the forest soil.

Listen child.
Love through the confusion.
Receive the beauty of life lived into Me
and crafted for an expectant soul.

October 22, 2012

Personal Focus

God, I don't even want to write for today was not a good day and I think every element played against my soul which is in contrast to yesterday's great connection. Today's pain revolves around hearing from a priest I respect, and the story about a person who lacks compassion and respect. From answering a question honestly, a student went into battle against two priests, but the issue oddly landed on my desk. Due to everything I have done to both fight for and respect the absolute need to receive the Eucharist, I'm tired. I've hit the point that I want to leave the Catholic Church for what it is doing in terms of overall leadership. If I long to receive that which You offer *[Body and Blood of Christ in the Eucharist]* and that which I am then called to be, the issue boils down to me as a person too. I am different and being hurt for all I cannot control or eat due to food intolerances. Even my boss is giving me a hard time. I feel let down and hurt by so many people and simply am trying to process the pain of life.

- What currently needs to "die" in your life?

- Are you resistant or confused about something that is causing you to not let go?

- *We must let go and accept death in order to allow transformation.* What can you imagine as new way of being beyond your current circumstance?

- In your life now, how is the Paschal Mystery* at work? Does internal confusion prevent you from letting go of something needed, to allow 'new birth?'
  The Paschal Mystery is a concept known in the Catholic Christian Church and proclaimed at every Mass. It is understanding that Jesus' life, death, and resurrection happens not only at Easter, but throughout our own lives. We each have to surrender things to "die" so new life comes.

Buried in Holiness

You are buried in holiness child,
steeped in a grace so strong that the flavor of your life
has no choice but to give praise back to My name.
In this all-encompassing love
there are consequences for the natural world.
As similar as the story of Eve
desiring to achieve greatness without first asking,
and in fact choosing to not trust,
you do trust, become feisty,
submit yourself all over again.
I have not forgotten you.
I know your deepest desires of your heart
(why does that scare you?)

Your desires are so blended that the response is timely to conceive.
Despite, and you just acknowledged this,
despite your longing for an equal partner/love
to walk with, you equally desire deeply
to remain intimate in love with Me.

Were mystics married?
Your heart knew the answer when the question arose –
the deepness and pondering of the life you so love
requires passion to be unmet in terms of surrender
to My Presence in and around you.
You cannot deny the lifeblood of your soul
seeking to serve in splendor the love I AM.
I have not forgotten. I have heard.
I have a plan. I always have a plan.

God to me on Feast of the Immaculate Conception
December 8, 2012

Personal Focus

It is important to explain the importance of the feast of the Immaculate Conception in the Catholic Church which honors Mother Mary's pureness at birth. It is a holy day of obligation as we look at her role to become the mother of God. She was set apart in holiness at conception, but she had to choose to live that holiness. Her will was always present and her will, and holiness, allowed her to give a yes to the Holy Spirit to become the mother of Jesus. This is but one reason why she is such an example for all Catholics and especially why this feast has always been so important to me and my prayer life.

[My entry] According to Your intention God, fill my being so the human loneliness does not cut so deep. I see the incredible gift of beautiful people in my life, almost all of which are not part of a daily walk with me. I am not getting what I want, but hope I am doing what You want. Help me to accept the [unknown] plan each time I struggle. The psyche is not a friend sometimes, it tells me that I am not important, and people don't care. I know they do but I believe I am easily forgotten. Why is that feeling so persistent?

- *Accepting God's plan is sometimes a daily struggle.* **What is it that you so deeply know, yet struggle against because you want something different?**

- **What hopeful plan of yours doesn't seem to match with God's plan?**

- **In the loss of your desire, how do you still love God through the pain of surrender or lack of acceptance?**

Faith of a Child

God's words to me (below) come at the end of my journaling conversation and sharing of extreme frustration! I also had been contemplating two phrases heard earlier in the day: Created to Praise. Chosen to speak.

You have not stumbled upon Grace child; you have been showered with an understanding which created your essence before you were born. The desire and depth of love in you, to remain in Me, has not left, allows you to stand in awe at moments in life others walk by and calls you to task to help or change.

In the most celebratory moments of prayer, when music rains from the heavens to wash doubt away and clear the stream to undivided love, you rest gently and freely praise. Words matter, to an extent that it uplifts you to transformed avenues of mystical prayer –coming into the presence of My love.

A child is not afraid, expects to be received, to be loved without cost, without any measure for what has been attained, simply created and chosen as life unto parent. A child thrives upon free-flowing, all-consuming love. In this flame of brightness, anything seems, anything IS, possible.

You have remained child unto Me in your soul, while the physical body has required other growth. The wisdom of the child is pure, undefiled grace, rooted in my playground of grace and effervescent love. In this knowing you were created to continue to praise and similarly chosen in your remembering to speak when others have forgotten.

I always use the unexpected to teach. From this place in time, though physical age in upon you, spiritual age is not. You still can see the world, in the eyes of splendid grace, the giftedness of Spirit runs deep in your veins.

You cannot fight Me and can be given strength to respectfully 'fight' others in a battle for light and truth. While truth stands and has been given, essence of a principle can remain true while circumstances around it can change.

You cannot ever deny Me in the Eucharist because you know tangibly that I exist fully, as an essence of great transformation in substance and in spiritual prayer. Your circumstances have etched into you a longing to want others to see Me as you do – an "intimate playmate" called to tend to the souls of others in unique ways.

What is it people need to hear? Your heart knows, it is how you choose to be heard and who can receive you. Your experiences of love, of union in Me, are the treasured gifts you do not hoard. Invite in those who can fully partake in the feast. Continue to wake others up! Patiently listen to where you are called next to teach in Spirit – in order to be received, not just to fight.

January 13, 2013

Personal Focus

In life we are sometimes placed in situations we do not want to be. Despite the pain we might be in, we are always called to remain in integrity to God in us even while those who are "Christian" around us force immense stumbling blocks.

- **When clouded by intensity of circumstances in life, or attacks to your character, how do you remember who you truly are?**

- **In life right now where do you need the "faith of a child"?**

Chapter 4
Learning from Nature

Whether you have time to take a walk,
or simply spend 5 minutes marveling in creation,
as you breathe open your ears to hear the glory of God.

If you ever feel disconnected, stop, and allow God's nature
to heal your soul and remind you of all you need.

Every piece in this section boldly proclaims the beauty of
the Paschal Mystery taught through God's creation.

Chasing the Sun

In the evening haze of life, a still shot is snapped
capturing the undeniable presence of satisfaction.
a day dawning upon a brilliant horizon
a moon rising to dance in the sky
the night breeze caressing the silence to come.

Stunned into simplicity
we are called to pause, reflect, give thanks
The abundance in our hearts furrows its brows,
"Not enough!" it proclaims,
"not enough grace to refuel our lives."

As we chase the sun to its resting place
beyond the unattainable moments of creativity
a longing grows in our hearts:
to be brilliant, awe-inspiring,
grace-capturing, all embracing
as a ray reaching every crevice
of sullen and joyful lives.

The chase to perfection remains –
the race not yet won,
(it never shall be the Son proclaims.)
The Son, all-knowing in a hidden way,
claims our hearts if we choose to look and remain.

Kairos time enacted -
we cannot chase the sun,
only revel in its beauty.

September 21, 2009

Prayer entry continued, words below are how I heard God.

So too, I revel in the beauty of your soul, your heart, your smile waiting to be filled with an all-encompassing, vital love that flows through all. Those open to receive, will receive. Those waiting, can be fulfilled. Those abstaining, are not forsaken.

You greet My love each day; allow Me to bid you goodnight; speak within the words of My Heart. It, My heart, knows your needs. When you cannot speak, the essence of you resides there within the safest confines of My being. You are birthed into greatness in your prayer of nothingness – though you feel lost without words. The satisfaction of stillness in your soul is peace that cannot be measured. The grace of My love is abundance in full.

Listen to your nudging. Be adamant about the need to reside here – you are needed to remain strong to support, give, nurture, claim, challenge, and love others. The openness to see creates unspoken gifts and also the emptiness of loss. You can feel full and empty in the same moment, just as you give and receive simultaneously in service.

Hear, sweet child, you cannot chase My love but only claim it for your life. May it grow into a brilliance that stops the world in its tracks. Be done child, done of your need to be incomplete. With Me, you are done and able to live completely in full love.

Personal Focus

This was all written in prayer time after I took a walk and felt like I was "chasing the sunset" trying to get a peek at its brilliance. God seeks our praise. In fact, we are created to praise, and nature gives us images to see God's handwork and be thankful. My last line before my poem and hearing God's response was: *"I have an inner need to be held and just snuggled with care. I forget how much energy can be put out [in presenting to a large group] and how much time it then takes to readjust my system. Still feel like there is a large missing piece, yet unnamed."*

- **What captured you today and brought a moment of peace, a smile, and awareness of God's grandeur?**

- **Have you ever received a direct response from God? If not, are you willing to ask? If yes, do you want that more often?**

- **How often do you feel you are chasing God's love rather than being open to receive His Presence wrapping around you?**

Sound of Prayer

The reciprocity of creation sustains the living breath of each soul.
Choosing to exist takes minimal effort.
Choosing to thrive requires constant connection
to the greatness of Me residing in you,
but also given and washed in moments of relationships.

Inhale the peace that floats in the air
which surrounds and enfolds your entire being.
When you forget, get lost, or distracted in your path,
I know how to lead you home.
Just listen and the sound of prayer will rain down upon you
with the lightness of butterfly wings.

As part of an existence which cannot be explained,
every moment teaches
every being proclaims
every person praises.
All in order to share and see an aspect of Me.
If I created all things and exist in all things,
You can never be apart from Me.

Prayer moves fluidly from one created thing to the next;
always exhaling the grace and beauty of Presence that sustains.

When you are immersed in prayer, you need not always speak.
Your heart is heard. I know you -
have known you – and will always keep you nestled
into the safest crevice of My being - a space solely your own.
Rest here. Remember.
Bring back this gift, these moments,
to those who are ready to hear.

October 10, 2010

Personal Focus

I walked in my "date place with God" [aka forest preserve] contemplating many things that happened at Mass. I once again struggled physically during Mass due to the depth of prayer in me. *"Once I received You (Eucharist) and could pray in the Spirit, my body could relax a little. We speak so much at these times and I desire to know what transpires. And there were tears, always seem to be, as I recognized things unknown to me and maybe long for what is not concrete, this depth with You."*

- What and who is your "sound of prayer" today - the moment that taught today, the person who spoke words of hope, healing, or encouragement?

- Even if it is only a few minutes of the entire day, where did you most see, feel, or hear God?

- What do you need God to remind you of today? How can looking into His handiwork of creation help provide an answer or some peace?

Surrender into Serenity

I have touched your heart with the depth of desire
flowing forth from the richness of life's opportunities.
In all you seek, in all you are,
a solitary step into stillness
necessitates the growth to follow.
Life is meant to be breathed into your soul
and given as an unfolding gift to others.
Yet groaning, or rather growing pains, do occur.

Seek Me in the splendor of the risen sky,
the glorious trees, the sounds of unspoken prayer
sung by creation serenading your steps.
As we walk, I share.

I infuse your being with love so grand,
you can only play vibrantly,
and then wrap this around your heart
before others take hold as wings are unfurled!

The flight of passion which speaks to the world
comes from time of stillness and surrender -
an openness to be claimed for the contingents of Christ's light
gifting the world with rich nectar of harmonious insight.

The struggle of the soul, of growth,
brings forth the serenity of gracious living.
Surrender into this serenity of life's tasks to accept all you are.

Birth to death.
Roots to wings.
Birds to flowers to colorful crispy leaves.
Is it not glorious how each moment can speak to your being
and teach untranslated lessons?

The pathway to one's soul
is hindered by the excess stuff of the physical world.
While the material world remains to feed and teach your soul,
choose your steps into the sacred path of our relationship.
You can only be loved into fullness of being.

September 22, 2011

Personal Focus

This entry was written after another beautiful fall "date with God" walking in the woods, admiring changing leaves, and seeking an answer to where I belonged as I looked to buy my first home. I walked in gratefulness for a dear friend and our conversation that morning, my new job, and passing on words of wisdom "of the process of letting go" to a young adult who lost her job. I wrote: "Our hearts are still weary of the goodness of the past mixed with the pain of being let go (or told no!)" It's tough to see, while walking in pain and stress, that something good will come.

- **What are the scenarios or questions in your mind today? Who do you feel you blessed today, or who blessed you?**

- **Where can you go in creation to release any stress into God's hands and heart *through His gift of creation*?**

- **As you move, observe, and listen to creation, can you allow yourself to release stress, surrender into serenity, and feel God's peace surrounding you?**

Posture of Prayer (when dust sparks life)

Pregnant moments of time call us to stop
and be aware of changes,
of fullness of life, joy, and yes even despair.
Simultaneously as we pause, the world waits with us –
prepares a home to offer back
and opens the secret door to our heart.

At times words will fail, cannot justify the magnitude
of passion and grace flowing within,
so we are called to lean *into* life
and rest with assurance of steps still to come.

When words betray the depth to offer
and objects appear too inconsequential
to help ease the burden,
the heavens open up and opposites occur:

The solid, rough wood of a tree
becomes the pillow to cuddle a weary soul.

The windy breeze causes you
to slow your step and take notice.

Uncertain tears flowing from stored pain
become nourishment for true growth.

A hand reaching out actually holds one up.

The dust of life then can spark light
because in the posture of prayer
nothing is too small to be used to bring glory to God,
to feel God's love transferring from one place to the next
because matter cannot stop
the incomprehensible flow of grace outpoured.
For, in prayer – in holy waiting – God waits IN us.

March 12, 2012

Personal Focus

I remembered walking on a different path a few days prior and seeing images that showed up in this writing. My journal entry of the day included: *You never fail to surprise me in abundant blessing with the path we [a friend and I] walk [being lay ministers in the Church]. Even if it is hard, I know there is a mutual shared path. I began my email response back to her with what I had heard and was pondering in prayer, 'when dust sparks light'. She has been sitting with that phrase and responded with all the little miracles which occur if we keep our eyes open. She gets You. I thank You constantly for that gift of being known, supported, and understood. How do we get through life when all situations seem too heavy? She asked me that, and in light of how well she heard the intensity of my events, my response went back to what I also heard from You on Saturday – the Posture of Prayer. There is no knowing or doing that could possibly suffice, just prayer.*

-   **What appears harsh and hurtful to you and yet offers an opposite stance of hope and healing?**

-   **When words can't describe how you are feeling, what helps you to express what is happening to those you love?**

-   **Sit with the phrases: *posture of prayer* and *when dust sparks light*. What do they mean to you?**

Fluid Motion

Nourished in the fibers of creation,
the stillness of symphonic sound washes me clean;
held in the presence of protected green and
moved by gentle winds of easy desire
I am cradled, rocked, and fed.

This time of soul reckoning comes with a cost -
loosening of my will means accepting Yours.
Within spaces of creative light and warmth, I do not waver.
Yet, upon my departure, hope wanes
and dissipates too quickly.

Do I, can I, stand solidly with You,
when a foundation of practical reality
screams a new path to a tired soul?
Thus engaged and caressed
in the fluid motion of expansive love,
how do I stand a chance?

To serve in, speak of, sing for Your name
has required a rebuilding of my being –
yet the willing building blocks of spiritual DNA
always existed,
tenderly waiting to be held in Your grace,
even when the running began – time and time again.

Knowing a tender sprout
can survive and thrive through severe storms
brings consolation that a questioning,
though solidly placed spirit
can thrive in unfriendly grounds -
only because I asked to be placed
where I would do Your will
and grow into the me You have sought from me.

Yet, while You have given roots,
at times I want the marathon.

I offered, trusted, and believed in goodness at the start.
All because of You.

Can You create the path of peace and ease needed to walk
and be healthy, at all levels, at the same time?

June 8, 2012

Personal Focus

My journal doesn't express the reasons yet shows the evidence of some inner stress about my own life path. Once again, wanting to feel valued and to thrive but feel too contained; love living alone but feeling too lonely and needing community which happens only when I reach out. And I wrote of a dream that really threw my mind (being in a car that was spinning out of control and was demolished – I made it out before the crash as did others, but no one could help stop the crash.) In dream interpretations, a car can sometimes symbolize your physical being, how you are "moving" through life. In my state of 'antsyness' I went out in a kayak that afternoon to enjoy "the surrender of silence, stillness and floating" to clear my mind.

- **What is God's will for your life? Has it changed throughout life or remained the same?**

- **If you are living what is your holy calling** (*your given vocation from God*) **do you ever wish you could do something different?**

- **How is God a part of your path and given credit for how you survive or thrive?**

- *Even if you are blessed with peace doing what you love, you still experience storms that might rock your foundation.* **What keeps you strong in trusting the giftedness of who you are in the world?**

Prayer in and of Creation

Ever conscious, yet uncertain,
of the ground upon which I stand
my spirit propels me forward
when circumstances hold me back.

Beholden with grace which is not my own
the trees beckon me to reach beyond and
pour forth the prayer begun within.

Words cannot, do not, capture the essence
of what is already captured in waiting cells
to be touched with the effervescent love of God
flowing through an open heart.

I do not seem to live for one.
Only through holy knowing do I realize and allow myself
to be and become prayer for all.
In this choice, a seeming culmination of loss of inner will,
the world around me prays with and within me.

Soaring strength of wings above remind of a freedom
which is innate, natural, and comes without a cost.
Heavy weight of broken branch
calls forth to me in surrender
to a new purpose, awaiting transformation.
Serenading spring of constant nourishment
calms the chattering beat of my soul.

In glorious sunshine and whispers of wind,
I soak into creation to be healed and be made whole again.
God's promise to me is thus, once again,
continually fulfilled.

September 14, 2012

Personal Focus

When I feel I cannot breathe, cannot speak the pain brewing inside, nor pull a friend into the depth of what is happening, I always go to nature to allow God to take it all and first restore me in breath so words might follow. This prayer walk and poem evolved from two weeks of intense personal stress/attacks and frustration at work. The day prior I wrote this: "Impressionable heart of my soul seeks out the Maker of my being for clarification of how to be and who I am. Words seem to muddle a comprehension of known existence which struggles in the mundane yet chooses to live and teach there. Is that me, really? I seem to be exhausted and confused at levels I don't expect. I feel disrespected and want to understand what is happening."

- **When you are "stuck in life" what, or who, restores you back to life?**

- **What, or who, reminds you of all you are and can still be?**

- **Where is God in this process for you?**

Blossom Benevolence

Reach into me to the places forbidden by mind's eye
which scream for attention in dreamlike stances of living.
Through blessed assurance of gentle gazes,
know me,
watch over me.

Let me know I am seen
so as to not be afraid of danger dancing within;
for the fire of emotions seem untouchable to me.
The strength You are can guide me into the fire
to be made whole again,
purified in crystalline waters of grace.

Swirling simultaneously from the anchor of the soul,
deception and truth coexist.
Itinerant grace holds both,
moves one to dissolve into the other.

Recognition now remains.
Knowledge of events, of named feelings,
accompanies the awareness of letting go – truth uncovered.
Sifting through of broken pieces must come,
or deception remains –
following the current in a swirl of unsanitary peace,
circling back round, again and again,
stuck by a forged yet faulty opened dam.

Should I but rest in Your presence –
be bathed in holy faith –
can stillness of sunshine,
sanctifying swells of song hidden behind leaf
and blossom benevolence fall upon me,
infuse into me all I need?

Amid deception and truth,
doubt and assurance also coexist,
tag-teaming the mind in dubious distractions.

Held by and living in You, I walk with my name –
Your identity – as my shield.

Surrendering to peace,
the covenant of Your love astonishes me once again.

The sun -Your Son, the colors - Your gifts,
circling together in creative form to be seen,
should I only look up to trust and receive.

May 13, 2013

Personal Focus

As I write this almost 7 years later, I can still vividly relive this day. I had a long slow walk, taking in every unique part of the path and seeing how it could teach me and help me process feelings. I stopped halfway to rest by a literal dam, praying to God to respond and give me peace from the painful situation I had just left but still scarred me. *[A year of stress and unhappiness at my job led to me leaving what I thought would be my 'forever job'.]* I think I spent 2 – 3 hours in the forest preserve that day seeking God's healing and inspiration for how to move forward.

- **When life not only hits, but pummels you spiritually to the ground, how do you choose to get back up and remain a peaceful presence to those around you?**

- **What in your past, or present, is asking you for healing? Have you asked God to take your pain to unburden your soul?**

Chapter 5
Leaning into Trust

*When life is complicated,
can you still hold peace
and trust that God is present?*

*Can you still praise (and pray to)
God amid the pain?*

Beyond Illusions to Grace

Graciousness of life is equal to the measure
of your innate ability to see beyond
the fine lines of truth and reality.
The passage you seek, though necessary for expansion,
is not an easy one to find.
The preparation can be arduous
or found in times of contemplation;
both avenues lead to still moments of grace.

Fed upon these divine moments,
your soul responds differently to all of life's circumstances.
You need to grow, but some choose
to keep the blinders of this life snapped on their eyes.
In this chosen distortion,
full moments of grace are not achieved.

One needs to open his or her heart
to see beyond the illusions of what is
and what is truly meant to be.
In the daily dyings and risings of life's moments,
the newness of life's discoveries can be found.

Blinded by judgment, one misses compassion
Blinded by solitude, there is refusal of love
Blinded by action, ('busy-ness')
miracle moments of peace aren't found.

Sealed in the goodness of My everlasting love
you each have possibilities to begin again, discover anew,
and see beyond the distortions of this world.
Choose Me. Choose love.
And, in all moments, the message of your heart will be clarified.
July 14, 2009

Personal Focus

Here is a summary of my journal entry: "Spirit God, I searched for You today, in need and in want of peace and understanding, and I could not reconcile my heart. I'm frazzled. I see things around me from loved ones from my perspective and wish we could all step outside of ourselves to better see all situations."

- **What illusions prevent you from truly seeing or accepting God?**

- **What judgements stop you from fully loving someone, even a family member?**

- **What moments are present to learn from, but you have turned a blind eye, not wanting the lesson?**

Enter into Presence

Softened into the mystery of undeniable grace
one stands in the Presence of God
and soaks in surrender to a plan guarded by angelic love.

It is your duty, your chosen call in life,
to enter into Presence,
seek the keys,
and unlock the splendid secret of your being;
to bring forth the holiness of My given love,
birthed into your being,
into all who can and choose
to speak of, know, and live in and for My name.

I do live in, through, and because of,
your heart, hands, and feet.
The effects of your life matter,
cause ripples which quietly extend into eternity.

The love and peace you choose to offer
matter more than you realize.
In simplicity of living,
known gifting of your senses and soul fed ways,
teach and feed others.

Break open your life. Allow grace to flow out.
In doing so, the essence of creative love can capture
aspects of life previously untouched,
even those off limits per your mind.

Hold My hand
as I hold and continually form your heart.
The world as you experience it
comes from your residing in Me,
in the comforting crevices of
evident, eternal, and expanding grace.

I do not leave you alone.
You are treasured and loved in unearthly ways.
Climb back into My lap child,
I will cradle you home for a time
to strengthen and renew your streams of life.
                                    ~Your Loving God~

                                    October 2, 2012

Personal Focus

Tonight, dear God, I need to collapse into Your Presence, which is the only definable place of comfort that I can name as a need to fill my being. The days have become uniquely intense which also means non-writable. Gramma almost went home to You. Last week is a blur due to Gramma's health and eventual decision for a pacemaker. And in all this, I'm still aware of a yearning to look at my life path, what I do and why I do it. Is there more I should be doing?

- **What are the keys that unlock all you really are in order to fully bring God's love into the hearts of those around you?**

- **Or, what are the keys you need to help unlock the pain of someone you love *to allow them* to have a glimpse of God's goodness?**

Reverent Joy

Struck with absolute surrender to come before a child,
to speak to a Deity from on high
humbled to human birth inside a silent soul;
the power is dazzling.

Awestruck with reverent joy,
the body knows what to do before the mind commands.
In prayerful submission, egos and attitudes fall to the ground;
one is stripped bare and seen for all he, or she, is.
Intimacy of present time conquers the wavering heart.
In time, all is made holy.

The journey to this place in time comes with choices
and a willingness to seek and search for the intangible;
find resonant glory in moments spoken to an untrained heart.

Gifts beholden in pure grace rain down to cleanse and renew:
Gold - the value of steadfast companions
Frankincense - the cleansing ritual of invited prayer
Myrrh - the sacred mystery
of tantalizing transitions to be treasured.

Hold the mystery and seek the manger;
for in your daily lives and in steps to come,
the simplicity of reverent joy can transform a soul
and call forth praise when tension too easily reigns.
Within the entrapment of physical beingness
lies a shimmering light,
brilliant, radiant, and dancing to be free.

To unlock the cavity of symphonic grace,
fall before the Child
in submission of love,
for this is the answer of My life,
what is called forth from you.

Allow Me to be held, loved,
treasured, cradled,
spoken to quietly,
that I may then do the same for you.

Light shining calls you, too, to live fully,
to also rise up in splendor to work with and follow Me.
Tasks of life come when necessary.
Acceptance given roots the soul.

Touch upon the radiance in others,
offer your hand, and remind their soul.

Teach those who cannot remember
and move forward should you ever have to let go.

As part of the brilliance of shining light,
nestle yourself into the swaddling love of Mary's grace.
Protection comes fully and is then painted onto the heart.

January 6, 2013
Epiphany Sunday

Personal Focus

The feast of Epiphany celebrates the wisemen who brought gifts to the baby king. Today's feast also calls forth the gift of our lives, how we show and present ourselves to God and to others. My entry spoke of some people who showed me the gifts I offer in my simple beingness and I named their gifts too. What remained on my mind was a question from our deacon: "Would you travel 10 months to 2 years simply to send 1 hour with a baby king?"

-   **What are the tangible gifts you offer?**

-   **What part of your ego needs to be released so you can lovingly hold our infant King?**

-   **What attitudes prevent you from showing up to praise?**

-   **What strengthens your inner light to produce reverent joy?**

Punctuated Prayer

In the silence you may speak,
scream the emotions of your heart
without words to acclaim the magnitude of your head,
but you must also listen -
to the instructions which seep into your cells,
into the spaces of uncertainty and fear.

Within the calm of My protecting love
you take a step forward,
not leaping into the unknown
but gaining strength to walk more solidly on your own.
The testing is almost complete –
though this is a term you do not like
nor do I portray (often,) it is most fitting at this time.
You understand.
The lessons are coming together
and therefore My will will also be heard.
I already see your future. It is good.

Those you love also secure this for you
as you are necessary to people
even though you feel quite dispensable.
Your light is stronger than you know.
Others are tested in your presence
and unexpected friction forms.
You could not stay.
You will dust your sandals (so to speak)
and shortly give up peacefully on your past.

Do punctuate your time of internal grieving
of processing ALL lessons.
There is a freedom which can come.
My role for you still remains,
is always two-fold in two worlds.

You are still a bridge.
Do not fear.
You can be accepted fully for the light you are,
so do not hide.
I equip you and hold your heart.
The time is present so listen.
Do be still.
Find your center and come often to Me.

May 24, 2013

Personal Focus

The prayers of the latter half of 2013 came from a long period of emptiness and pain – grieving a decision that had to be made and yet trying to understand the purpose of it. Everything can teach – when we are ready to see. My entry prior to hearing God was trying to tackle the loss of not only a job, but the people at the job I genuinely cared for and felt connected to. I tried to remind myself, by writing names of friends, that while I don't have people around me all the time to help comfort when I feel in need, the people in my life aren't superficial and will be present when they can.

-   **When you are upset with life, or God, what stops you from showing up in prayer and pouring your heart out to Him?**

-   **What things have you gleaned from tough times in life? What (if any) difficult situations are you currently in need of learning from?**

<u>Strength of the Summons</u>

Summoned into captivating spaces,
come into full response of trust into My heart.
It is here in undivided attention
where I can reach into, and teach, your soul.
You, child, are not lost. Hear me well.
The world around you provides such distractions
to a soul yearning to work in My embrace.

Would I lead you to a place that could harm your soul?
The past hurt, but could not touch the vibrancy of your soul,
nor your gift to the world.
Your lesson of strength fully received -
the next place is then prepared.

Your friend remains,
her walk will look different, too, as pieces settle.
When you are present there, hold the grace and love which pours
through. People pray for you, too, albeit quietly at times.
Your team of supporters, known and unknown, still exist.

Prayer fills spaces without need of knowledge or words.
As you gift this peace to others in looks and song,
souls unite momentarily
to lift in unconscious hope of promises to come.

All are not awake there
and your space to hold in tandem with [a friend]
is to stabilize the force of love which can flow
in the centerpiece of prayerful life.

You look surprised, but you have always known.
As you stay, you can quietly affect more people.
I cannot offer you the proof your heart and mind desire,
too many choices are still to come.
This peace you have when we speak, hold tight to this.

You are so far from being done in ministry.
Your friend is right, the Catholic Church needs you,
needs both of you, to shine gloriously in joy.
Be strength and witness for others and yes, for each other.
The journey is unique and neither is it complete.

June 22, 2013

Personal Focus

I came to my prayer journal sharing the struggle of my heart (the job loss and what to do with my life) and yet gratefulness for the support of my parents coming in town to support me and even pray over me after I had cried. The angst in my soul was wanting to trust God fully and yet not lose things that grounded me (my new home and even other colleagues in my field as I feared not working in ministry would mean a loss of common ground.)

- **What helps you to garner strength in the middle of struggles?**

- **In what ways does God speak to you so you can hear/receive the strength He intends for you?**

- **In what situations might you need to trust God more so that, even in hard times, you can name God's gifts or blessings?**

- **When you feel heavy with despair, do you doubt the goodness God created in you? What helps you accept God's plan for your life?**

Tandem Dance

Through the sifting of time, feet are lodged in sands
waiting for footprints to be danced into action.
The rhythm of movement requires faith
in hands which guide and hold you close.
Falling into the treasured capsule of falling sand,
your choices coalesce with known hopes and fears,
all seen through the eyes of the Designer of your heart.

Speak often while trusting in Perfection offered from My hand.
I still hold you close.
We still dance in tandem, even while you rest.
This is not a time to give up hope.
Your cells are primed with love –
knowledge your mind has yet to put into words.

Immerse yourself into the glory of My grace
still raining upon you and
holding you together.

I am the Author of your life,
Creator of your heart,
Designer of your dreams.
If you believe this to be true,
your only choice then is to come and trust.
Lean into Me.
Listen well to the heartbeat of Love.

July 4, 2013

Personal Focus

The thoughts written just before the response are telling. "My steps for tomorrow are unknown and I am offering up my path once again as I feel conscious that some doors could be closing, even though my heart likes the options! Waiting in the unknown remains scary and the peace I have, at times, also crazy for the steps I walk. Create and offer me quickly (my version of quick please) that which best suits where I am to be to serve and grow."

- **When life is complicated and your hopes and dreams crushed** *(in life or a situation)*, **what is your "level of trust" with God? During those times what prevents, or allows, your heart to still turn to God?**

- **Do you see Him as "leading the dance of your life" or are you commanding the steps? If needed, what steps can you take to change who is in charge?**

Dear World,

I am part of the whole of humanity seeking to bring forth a transformation of life, to open doors for true love, complete light, respectful comprehension of what binds us together. The massive acts of senseless violence and pain hurt me, tear at a soul which is given by and given back to God; yet is connected to each person I love deeply and even those I do not know. I listen in an ineptness to understand hatred, yet knowing hatred exists and hurts humanity.

Is the cost of self-preservation, the need to be the best, the desire to cause pain minimally by words, harshly in actions, and strongly in deadly violence, the answer? There has to be a better way. There is a better way, but we are afraid that the act of doing nothing is seen as weakness, that trusting God makes us powerless.

Yet, when we lack answers, we turn to each other, to the God we know individually and collectively, to cope. Cannot this same Being of Love, the Creator of all, be cause for strength to survive on days without severe pain? Could not the Light of God be shone brightly in us, each day, to no longer be blind to the pain of others? To act as neighbors with a heart, not strangers with cause for concern?

We have grown so large, so far from where we came. Distractions come in beautifully wrapped gifts when the most beautiful gift we need to treasure passes by unoffered – time to live, love, be with others in harmony, and treasure deeply those in our midst. A tragedy makes people who survived, who see and feel the pain of lives lost and families grieving, hold their loved ones closer.

Within the newfound love and need to hold close, stronger walls of protection are being formed. Fear is ignited within. Are we ever truly safe? The essence of your life breath is your key, and when breath is taken from us, we perish. This happens in many ways beyond the physical act of dying. We hold our breath as we live – control our way of being and living. Inhale the gift of life so you can exhale the love and strength given to be your light, your gift in the world. We are each one; but one person, one moment, affects eternity.

As such, knowing we each affect the other, whose "rights" are more important? Whose "needs" to be satisfied most appropriate? The avenues to act violently exist. *The graces to live as love placed in the world are strong if we are each brave enough to return to the roots of our lives*. Laws are crafted, weapons fortified, walls erected. Consider and then do what is necessary to create (rather listen to an innate knowing and given Word in many forms) rules which force actions of intentional grace. *May weapons of the heart shoot out compassion, mercy, joy, and forgiveness*. Walls be pliable so as to create more space in our lives to love…not less.

When we start to act as that from which we were meant to be in this world, containing the ineffable grace of God to give to others, there is a chance for change.

Hoping in tear-stained love.
Me

December 16, 2012
after the shooting at SandyHook Elementary School

Personal Focus

The letter speaks for itself; I came to my prayer journal to process pain with God and ended up writing to the world.

- **What words do your heart scream, wanting to make a difference in the constant life tragedies and horrific acts of violence that plague our world?**

- **If you are able, write your own letter** (or create a vlog or live video post), **addressing the problems of the world and share how you wish it could change.** Make sure to be honest about the change and justice needed, but also prayerfully bring God our Creator, Jesus our Savior, and Holy Spirit our Advocate into your message of prayer.

Chapter 6
Choosing to Gift Praise

Prayer is multifaceted.
It's a time to plead, find peace, and praise.

Prayer time with God is for seeking direction,
speaking needs, and silencing the ego mind
to surrender our truth to God's Truth.

Prayer is God hugging us and yet it is also us hugging
God in thanks for what He gives us in those around us or
just letting our soul speak love letters of praise to Him.

A Soultender's Prayer

Flow through me
effortlessly
meticulously
that particles unknown may be covered
drenched
in grace that transforms
and enlightens the path to walk
now, and the future steps to come.

Enrich my will
with a heart that seeks Yours
holds out to receive Love
to offer this and in return
unearth the avenues of how to exist as
a child of Your Presence;
to invite others to an eternal resort
of effervescent joy
to escape
to praise.

Should You but allow me to see glory shining
ignite the flame
and call me to pillars of light so that
we can simultaneously sustain grace
be charged in creativity
and carry the conception of humble Truth of Love
to become manifested at Your will.

Fortified in Your heart, through witness
and devoured in protection of fluid praise
I
we
shall tend the souls who dance into our midst
and return our hearts
our souls
back to Your care.

September 15, 2013

Personal Focus

In my entry I wrote about reading this theological, yet metaphysical book: *The Holy Trinity and the Law of Three: Discovering the Radical Truth at the Heart of Christianity* (Cynthia Bourgeault.) My mind was pondering much of that depth coupled with my life and need to find new focus/purpose. *"Through this [book] I have thought about 'those in my clan,' of similar souls who are blessed, and the unearthed vision of a community living together to share and prosper. Not certain why but I heard this name of this unknown group as 'Gabriel's Breath'. Through Gabriel You spoke to Mary so Spirit could be breathed upon her openness to be the vessel to allow You to grow and expand. It is receptivity to the unknown gifts in our lives that brings forth such beautiful movement."* And then suddenly I wrote this prayer "Soultender's" which I loved and surprised me.

- Who are the people in your spiritual community who truly live and call forth the light of Christ within you? Do you spend enough time nurturing those relationships?

- Who are the people you are called to mentor in discipleship? How are you being called right now to share your light more actively and thus be a "soul-tender" to another?

- Reflect on Mother Mary, her constant yes to God. How can you allow her witness of trust, love, and faith to be a model for you?

Candlemas Prayer

Treasure of Light inexhaustible,
fill my soul with your holy fire.
Ignite within me
a passion for serving a call
which claimed my name at birth.
May radiant warmth of your blazing flame
inspire avenues for action to be a witness
and hope in silence
to renew the path to be your disciple.

In the barren attitudes surrounding me,
may flickers of light spark their own
to come see the vast wealth
found in this mysterious,
yet soul-filled and joy driven, path.

For already dancing flames of depth and desire,
may we unite together in essence of Your love
and dance into a shared freedom
to honor and praise
the wisdom in the gift we know and
acknowledge by serving You.
Help us to surrender our fears
and breathe in Your grace,
to grow strong in Your love,
to see and seek Your presence in our lives,
and be this presence
of hope, of light, for one another.

February 2, 2014

Personal Focus

My prayer was the only part of my heart. February 2nd is Candlemas day which is celebrated differently in different cultures. In the Catholic Christian faith it is the day Jesus is presented in the temple for the first time, the day Mary is purified after giving birth, and also when a righteous and holy man, filled with the Spirit, Simeon, and the prophetess Anna, proclaim immediately who Jesus is. In some cultures, candles are blessed on this day. For several years, I would give gifts of candles to a few people who greatly aided my spiritual journey that year. No doubt all of this was on my mind when I came to prayer, along with wondering how to help others be strong in faith!

- How is your overall relationship with Jesus? Is it burning bright, flickering in uncertainty, or igniting hope in others?

- What helps you stay ignited in the faith walk? What do you need in order to be a stronger light?

Precipice Prayer

Infuse into me inspiration
Hope which is not my own
Security which cannot be offered
only gleaned
in the aspects of brevity
in a clasp of hands -
formidable in love
an essence of everlasting covenantal growth

All leading me
to the precipice of chosen holiness
while tumbling back down into
reveled reality of argumentative tears
and the masterful labyrinth of living
still woven, wound, whittled
into Your merciful grace

March 24, 2014

Personal Focus

"My prayer this evening has been intense and also shared with three gracious strongholds, all who heard about my head and heart; how I feel conflicted given a predicament at work. (Someone being accused of improper touch.) Advice given by one friend was a quote [not sure who wrote this.] *'Between the past and the future is the holy now. Be here. Exist in the mess. Name it for what it is.'* ...Trust is a concept between a right and a wrong way. You are not a concept or theory. In my being You are necessary and a needed reality. While I do not speak in lofty ways, may who You are in me be known to teach others to make a difference."

-   **What are your pleas to God right now?**

-   **What does security mean to you at this time of life? Where does your security come from?**

-   **When you experience difficult emotions – stress, angst, doubt, fear, uncertainty– can you still have trust in God to keep you wound in His care?**

-   **If you are an artist, how might you draw this prayer? If you aren't, step outside your comfort zone and see what you can create.**

In service of Triduum

Beckoned to posture of prayer,
soul spoke silently, effortlessly
to assure each living cell
of a duty ascribed long before choice settled in.

As the heart dispersed the clarion call of absolute existence,
knowledge and conscious desire took place.
Soulful living, service in giving -
clouded by emotions of intensity -
the road divided in options of gifted movement
to sit in the mess
or bypass the disaster to create safety for others.

In doing the latter, a new journey of prayer develops;
one not crafted intentionally, but rather
opened in surrender to serve willfully.

Triduum service speaks to me,
allows one to be present,
(when presence does not seem enough)
to prayerfully wash feet and hearts,
(without use of cleansing water)
to share in a feast of life,
(when emotions spilleth over)
to sit in holy silence - desired surrender,
and to listen in clarity and speak in certainty
(when conversation alone is too daunting)

Of not my own plan is this call
rather for service of another, (of others)
to prayerfully craft or participate in gifts of past
and to peacefully hold the present
with the path of Christ in the center
not my will be done, but Yours.

In service of Triduum treasures
matter beneath my feet -
flowing in my heart -
feels foreign, yet equally comfortably known and accepted.

Through a heartbeat of reverberating Love,
my cells group in unity
to hold all in reverent awe of the One
and similarly *in one*
who provides the sustenance of Triduum living.

April 18, 2014

Personal Focus

There is a term in Celtic spirituality called *kything* where one soul can pull on another to pray and receive support without that person necessarily being conscious of the need (though sometimes a pull to check on a person suddenly comes.) My friend, for whom I wrote this, also works for the church as a Director of Liturgy and Music. Talking with her for the past 15 years, there is always a deeper understanding of our shared difficult walk to be a lay minister in the Church.

The Triduum (Holy Thursday, Good Friday, Easter Vigil) is the most amazing part of the liturgical year for the Catholic faith. It is equally exhausting for those who help at this 3-day Mass. I love being present to pray and sing at each service, but also to prayerfully support her. This specific year I felt an even stronger pull to be present, to pull her into my prayer in adoration.

My entire entry spoke of my incredibly deep and filling soul conversation with God and being gifted many clear visions, or images, to help me understand my current path, but also how to help my friend. That year, I was in service to her without deep conversations, just soul/heart knowing.

- **Who are you called to serve in friendship, in prayer, in willingness of being present *even if* you can't easily talk or know the details of what is causing stress?**

- **What are ways you show up to Jesus to be fortified in faith?**

Soul Breaths

Entrenched in dignified battles for grace,
these times exude the nutrients of blessed living
and tie the hearts together, one to another,
seamlessly stitched by My hand of generous care.

Your braces of living are known, blessed, and chosen.
Continue to be pulled into the
exhales of trusted Presence,
as words flow and strength feeds the spirit.
I come unknown, yet am discovered
in such simplified moments -
Grab these!

Hold intangible heart wisdom close to you.
Allow communities of love to grow, for these are necessary
and never in the ways you most expect.

Test your feet upon the waters,
for trust is tenuous in the soul, yet rich in movement.
You cannot see, will not know, and must feel.
Passion erupting within ignites with reason.

Be unafraid of this power.
The chalice of known Spirit is burning in your being:
catalyst for change,
catalyst for hope.

May 4, 2014

After my conversation and sharing in the prayer poem, I heard God speak clearly to me.

You seem to doubt the effectiveness of your ways, yet when you are open – when you focus on a reason or a face, a purpose, and My grace – all comes. The bricks will be broken. The work is difficult, but do not falter. There is purpose, reason, and hope.

As you name your stalwarts of faith, make sure to be one – covering yourself in the precious substance of prayerful space. Your head needs to be quiet, but we need this space now. The tide has to change on all the accounts you seek.

Dive back into gentleness to rescue the greatest armor to your soul – gentle dignified strength. In order to have this, you need to be back in yourself. You are not. You slip out unknowingly and have been dragged through a tarry mud. Clean your spirit in My waters of deep, healing, peaceful grace that are washing over you. Then you won't feel so lost. These nights coming are long and late, but short moments here will keep you centered and strong. I know your prayers: let them go and speak your truth.

Personal Focus

The background for my prayer this Emmaus Sunday came after two Masses at two churches and conversation with two good friends. All to help me calm down from the explosive stress of the past week with a few volatile situations at work. I wrote May 3rd "This is unending and entirely unnerving – I do not engage into a world outside this mess (tv news), which isn't good, yet I cannot even handle my own life stress well." I wrote a number of prayers for my boss, people at my work parish, other friends and their needs, and my needs to be able to do what I was asked to do at the parish.

To act as a catalyst for change means resistance and unintended pain for others may follow. Gifted strength in life comes from how grounded we are in God and in those who are our "braces" who help us continue our walk.

- **What are you called to do now that seems impossible?**

- **Who, or what, helps you move through what seems to be immoveable to allow positive growth to occur?**

- **When you know you are doing what is right, but others hit back hard, how do you keep the integrity of your soul?**

Fallow Ground of Grace

Breathe into me sustaining grace
a melodic strength of incomprehensible wisdom
to seek beyond the chaos
and artistically dance into a patience not yet known.

Color my soul with endearing love
a radiance of light gifted in Spirit
to pull out the kindness in others
when their armor and pain pins and nails me back
and depletes the humanity within me.

Enrich a searching soul seeking to do Your will
with sustenance from Your heavenly court
morsels to feed the cells shivering in Your Presence.

As unknown beings step into a field,
that terrifyingly beautiful fallow ground,
equip me with the eyes to see their role
to plant faith, fertilize glory, water the doubting,
and offer in my presence
the astonishing depth of Your Light
to replenish and allow them to thrive.

Grounded and moved in rhythm with Your love,
the task in manageable.
May moments where pain and denial pull me away
lessen as Your will continually becomes my joy.

May 22, 2014

Personal Focus

Today's prayer was the only entry. The events of the whole month (volatile situation at work) had just barely calmed down. The title of this prayer began the day before when I wrote: "fallow ground is terrifyingly beautiful." The best way to explain what I did, really was asked to do, was to "kill" a beloved program for teens that was good for them in social and psychological support. However, it had nothing to do with Catholicism or helping teens connect to God, in fact at times it even bashed God, yet was run by our Catholic Church. The teen leaders were great people, yet once I had to stop this yearly event, these same teens who I wanted to empower to lead similar events but with a God focus, hated me. All I did was necessary but took courage. I could see a hopeful future if they could let go of anger. They couldn't.

Look back to the bolded phrases in the prayer.

- **Which phrase do you most need to pray with this day?**

- **What is your need to be shared with God?**

- **How do you assess the "farmland" of your life and what changes/enhancements might it need? As in, where might you feel you most need God's grace to fertilize part of your life?**

Soul Providers

Soul Providers, tested in firmament of faithful walking,
the path strewn with softened sands of grace
and edged rock of unseen ways,
steps still come
slowly and solidly,
assured in moments of Divine grace

Embraced- entrenched rather- in blinding mist,
it is a Voice which called us to life
that propels the life momentum forward

Standing still in denseness
exempts us from growing –
a promise our hearts proclaimed willingly at birth
with blessed desire to serve
and match the manna given
presence in another
prayer in solitude
praise in community

In the midst of great movement
new life springs forth,
wings unfurl with majestic glory
and light within finds a purpose to shine, to give.

August 28, 2014

Personal Focus

Another prayer coming out of my writing of life events as I shared about hopes to heal some past personal pain for me. I also prayed for a soul friend and her intentions as she was silently dealing with things but called upon me (that kything term) to help support her spiritually.

- **Who/what helps you move forward in life?**

- **Who/what encourages you in faithful living to accept the call of discipleship?**

- **Who/what helps you to hear God when you are confused?**

Chapter 7
Singing Soulfully

*Music heals, inspires,
pulls out emotions and enhances joy.*

*Can your prayer life be musical in nature,
aiding to the praise God deserves?*

*How often do you claim and name
the awesome nature of God?*

Grandeur of God

When one is charged with the grandeur of God
and the spring of joy has been found again,
the only thing left to do is to lift your arms up and praise.

Praise the Spirit of God and the Spirit of Truth -
the essence of life that flows in our veins,
and spread this energy ~
this passion for life ~
back into a pulsing world that needs to relearn how to pray;
a world that needs to learn to be still
in the center of each precious life.

In each and every life there is a connection of peace,
a possibility to light up the world.
Connect those spots, fill the hole
and raise the world in love.

God's grandeur, our splendor,
comes forth in unique, passionate, and even simple ways.

We are called to listen to this Truth,
to listen to our God,
one and whole in communion...in Eucharist with all~
not just our community, family, and home;
but in solidarity with all to praise and pray this gift of life
to the groaning of the rest of the world.

Be at peace. Use your gifts.
Become the healers you already are.
Blaze a trail of joy & light
that spontaneously will erupt
into a life-giving fire of hope.

September 2006

Personal Focus

If I recall correctly, this wasn't a journal entry, but something that came to mind in the middle of a chiropractor session. Once I finally had access to paper, the thoughts were quickly scribbled down and then typed. This is a prayer message that always makes me smile.

- **What do you do with the grace given to you that is meant to be shared?**

- **How do you boldly or quietly "sing your praise" into the world?**

- **What areas of your life, your family, your friends, *need* something only you can offer?**

Wrap your Soul in Song

There are implicit sounds of grace exploding in your soul;
each tenured note chosen to inspire a new strand of wisdom.
In the busy-ness of life, music holds the background,
the skeletal existence of spiritual knowledge,
alive but not yet intensified.

Embraced by melodies of serene beauty,
the soul will pause to inhale the grace
and sing a note back to feed the world.

Your soul cannot remain quiet for long;
silence and stillness must naturally
coexist with fullness and noise.
Precarious balance is vital
to preserve the steadfast rooted love
anchoring the soul into one realm of existence
to be brought down and experienced by others.

Both levels of knowledge are needed -
loftiness of idyllic love and
rootedness of treasured wisdom.

You would do well to listen
to the movements which occur within
and walk in the direction of love coloring your life
through prescribed moments of personal giftedness; –
times crafted uniquely for each person,
yet times are also shared in community.

Seek these times.
While you can dance alone
and song energizes and lifts the sinews of your being,
proclaim, too, together.
The cleansing prayer of musical presence
and joyful dance offers perfect praise.

Seek Me in the tender moments
and be held in times of pain and confusion,
the melodies of chosen grace live within you.

When cells and memory are dulled to the senses,
stuck in a cycle of inner fallacy,
certain sounds will unlock the door
and allow peaceful notes to serenade the soul
into a glorious embrace of My true Love.

Believe I Am.
I Am in all, of all, and will work through all
if I am accepted and chosen within.

Whether in softness of jeweled lullabies
or full-throated praise,
I am praised and offer love back to you.
Continue to live in me, sing of Me, dance in My arms.
Praise of the soul lives on for eternity
and secures your place to come in the heavenly chorus.

January 20, 2012

Personal Focus

My entry started: "Gentle God of the dewfall of our lives, Your touch is both necessary and gifts us with the unexpected in our lives. This week seemed exceptionally long and yet there were moments which so filled my soul with your grace." I then spoke of people and conversations that were so helpful, ending with a note of thanks for my friend who sang at Mass and loving her ethereal voice. As I prayed, music wrapped around my soul. I needed music to feed my soul that day and found it in a variety of ways.

Think about God's love and grace as a song.

- **What kind of song would it be for you? What genre? Which artist sings it? What kind of instruments are present?**

- While honoring and protecting our soul is needed, giving others the love of God through us is also needed. **What is the "volume" of your faith for others to "hear" your song?**

Spirit Dances *(Feast of Pentecost)*

Oh gracious child who sleeps in My womb, the wonders of the earth lie within you to reach into the depth of your cells and feed you the fullness of My created vision. In seeing the glory your eyes are open to states accessible to hearts aglow with love for My heart.

The Spirit which resides within you speaks when spoken to, teaches when called upon, and dances in freedom with permission from others; all knowing gifts learn to respect the limit accepted by those who choose to receive. To tap the power and act as the vessel for which you serve has never been a simple task but the joy which glows from you is rich in ways unfathomable and untamed by others. You are unstoppable; a beautiful force of light to be reckoned with as you do not want to be contained, know the wisdom of Angelic love and tender grace protecting your being.

As the sun shining can only be received with one's eyes at its dimmest hour, know this for the gift you are and need to be. In simple moments beauty explodes and peaceful serenity comes, stopping those in sight and halting all motion. As a blessed chosen one, a servant to My call, you are learning and continuing to struggle – never turning away from Me. You cannot exist apart from My Presence and for this you sing in absolute abandon and turn in tears through stress and misunderstanding of others.

You cannot lessen your light but can cloak the radiance so as to be acceptable to those near. When quiet permission sustains your soul and grants acceptance, you play, and carry others to a higher light; a knowing of love which is attainable for all, but not acceptable for full living as it demands change.

Your life, the world, is changing. The demands of one in power threaten to extinguish the life force necessary for soul survival. It is easy for you to come uninhibited, not so for others. But you remind them of the possibility to skip into easy pleasure in My grace. The political powers that be threaten to demolish standards of free-flowing grace. To "win" in the battle be at peace in Me and knowledgeable of all within you. The experiences in the past few weeks have taught you great deeds. Peaceful surrender is not laying down to another's will but allowing Me to move in You with words and actions to help others. Remain open to Spirit existing strongly in you, speaking clearly to console and serve.

You are seeking an answer, an understanding to your prayer this weekend. Can it be all neatly intertwined? For the sufficiency you seek, not so. For My purposes glory is attained even while you cannot express this in words. You began last night; you listened enough to know and yet matters perplex you; a wall erected stopped your friend. Accept your role as it is – for all you love and who meet you are teacher and friend. Your soul dance does have a journey with hers – it is easier for you to believe others gift you than for you to accept how you gift them. Yes, hold this to be true enough for you to realize that all is caught, considered, and tucked into corners unspoken and unreachable in another, yet momentous nonetheless.

ST is riveted in the future grace of doing and yet not all can quiet themselves down enough to feel My tender touch. The place, the community at large, seeks promise of prayer to transform and that they do. The rules of institutional matters rejected creates a slight imbalance in how to move forward into the needed lessons and workings of life. Conversely SR as a community at large follows rules so closely that Spirit does not move as freely, cannot tap dance creatively into the congregation.

Prayer is not about perfection. Prayer is about presentation of one's life – their mind, heart and soul – given freely, willingly. In this matter some at SR need much movement, those (some) at ST feel the gifts of movement and need to learn how to integrate this into their personal life. You are not the middle ground child – Spirit seeks to be seen in you. At times ST feeds *you, some, but is not entirely enough, for in receiving one must then give.*

My message was, and is, clear. Go out and preach. Be My hands and feet. Breathe life into others. Hidden in the upper room no work can get done. And while you cannot force all to pray and praise as you do, you are called, specifically, to trust in the goodness I have placed in you.

You know Me deeply and want to share this fragrant love with everyone who knows Me at their level. The most exciting event of life cannot be hidden or kept quiet, [just as] the Spirit at work in You presses others into action. Be not afraid to be YOU no matter the cost, yet simultaneously utilize wisdom and knowledge to know when too much is too much.

Stepping on the hidden plain,
the masterful plan of created dance is present to enrich the soul.
Timid in actions, fluid gifts are given
to revitalize the body and renew the soul.
Movements are known by all there, not taught.

Gliding into grace innately enriches the community.
As one, but separate, the dance cannot be seen alone.
Trust the guidance of those on your left;
Share the splendor of risen love with those on your right.
Never ending, the Spirit unfolds,
grows into consciousness, and can be unstoppable –
only if the community as a whole moves together.

Learn the dance of your soul.
The song is found in the life of a friend;
harmony received from rituals offered (and shared);
rhythm sustained by those who teach us discord...
One body, one Spirit, one Love, one heart.
A dance for many, the song for all.

May 28, 2012

Personal Focus

The Feast of Pentecost for the Catholic Church ends the 50-day Easter season, celebrates the birthday of the Church, and reminds us to honor the gift of the Holy Spirit given to us to live our faith as Jesus said. I love this feast! I absolutely love the Holy Spirit; I love celebrating that the Spirit comes to empower us to live our faith; I love singing the gorgeous holiness and strength of the songs! This specific celebration, I ended up at 3 Masses, 2 at one parish, and 1 at another – both are places I like to worship, but there are great differences. I was so very aware of many things that day and wrote of my ponderings. As shared first, God responded, and His response was the best way to share what came before the small prayer poem.

- **What kind of faith community do you belong to? Are you a spectator in the community, an active participant, a leader?**

- What do you think about this line: *"Prayer is not about perfection. Prayer is about presentation of one's life – their mind, heart and soul – given freely, willingly."* **Is it applicable to how you pray or even think about prayer? Why or why not? What holds you back?**

- God shared: *Hidden in the upper room no work can get done.* **Do you hide your faith, your gifts, your talents? If so, why? How _do you_ specifically share the goodness God placed in you?**

Dancing with Spirit, Rooted in Light

I have held you up as a tree to stand and offer witness that growth is possible, strength is constant, and resilience is never ending in a spirit rooted in My love. In the sight of unknowing and seemingly uncertain free-flowing and gentle strength, majesty and awe fill a person willing to receive grace. Others are rocked to their core and guard their timid reserve, placing feigned power over serenity of peaceful observation. Your former boss has done both with you, seen all you are and fought against this natural beauty while also recognizing the truth of what is there too. You dance to remain in Spirit. He stands in solitude seeing a dance he knows but does not participate in.

As you have tried unconsciously in the past, and out of sheer frustration in the present, you cannot remain asleep. I will constantly wake you up; tell you to rise and stand as shining light and beauty to others. This is not easy because you are a warrior while also being a child.

To love unconditionally, not seek fighting, and desire to rest in Presence and play with angels means the "opposite" side struggles. Precisely because your soul is etched into the depth of My light, you are given strength and a faith which will never die.

Broken? No. Wounded? Yes. Tend the scars and create the ointment to then treat others. TRUST in Me. I am not leaving you alone and you will get through the current battle "in-tact."

All-Present God and Protector of your soul
July 1, 2012

Personal Focus

My entry spoke about the celebration of the 50th anniversary of SR and my joy in our ability to have an amazing choir concert to celebrate the spirit of the parish. Yet, it ended with my pondering about a former boss who went to SR and how I still struggled figuring him out. While I had forgiven him, I still didn't trust him; was skeptical and wondered why he had the conversation he had with me.

- **What kind of roots do you feel you have in God's love?**

- **What struggle are you facing (or have faced) that might be used to help others?**

- **Are you cautious about sharing the depth of your life to others? Or, can you use pieces of your life to help evangelize or encourage others in their faith walk? How?**

Secured Soulfulness

Invisible layer of sheer love
blankets the aura of beingness which walks alongside.
Steps are not, will never be, fully owned

Yet could a perceptive heart still believe?
Fathom to embrace the graciousness
of unending Presence
and gifts to secure the necessary armor of life?

Within the fortitude of complete surrender,
to an inability to survive singularly, the softness of wings
tread tenderly,
touch truly, and
teach thoroughly.

Love is palpable.
Prayer is present.
Friends at a distance secure safely
the soulfulness which remains in me.

August 2, 2012

Personal Focus

On July 29th I wrote a prayer asking God to: "repair my heart in the crevices of space steeped in uncertain doubt and fear of an inability to be known and loved. Help me find or create the community I seem to seek to better know and live my path in You." I was dealing with the emotions of finalizing a piece of letting go of a past job I loved, not feeling cared for, or connected to friends, and my Gramma was struggling in her health. I was overwhelmed. It took a few days, but a reprieve came August 2nd to feel known and heard. This prayer poem was my way to acknowledge the gift of an answered prayer.

-   **In a personal struggle, who becomes your "battle gear," the person who most helps you fight or regain your sense of balance and trust back in God?**

-   **When you feel totally alone, how do you cope through challenges or feelings that seem insurmountable?**

-   **Can you note times you have prayed to God and, relatively quickly, found a response to your prayer? How did that help strengthen your relationship with God/Jesus?**

Fashioned Praise

Celebrated in the midst of the people,
the vibrancy of dance and echoing of song
transform (at least can) space and time
to tug upon the corners of sleeping souls
and call forth unified worship and praise.

Fashioned entirely within the prayers of the people, I rest,
re-gifting creation with an attribute of holiness
to carry forth from this place a resolution to be made new,
to live closer to one's chosen call to be a blessing to the world.

Hearts awakened sing willingly,
while slumbering souls seek sustenance to choose to change.
All are in this journey in unique phases,
the resolute desire of transformative prayer still remains.

Thus, greet one another in holy praise.
Sift through the distortions of the day, and
place the conscious and collaborative choice
of our union as center of all.
Life gifted.
Prayer walking.
Community driven.

In this I await the goodness which has already claimed your life.
Listen to the stillness of hope, and strength of peace
to continually refashion the avenue of grace
given and gifted for this moment of time.

+God+
September 16, 2012

Personal Focus

"I don't know how to address You tonight in poetic praise of soulful gratefulness. You are my restorative God whom I turn to, live in, abide in, and seek profusely. As I discovered once again, the child in me desperately needs union with You on many levels. I needed the depth of prayer this weekend at Mass – a visual gift of profound embrace with conversation* I do not control, yet occurs, and my entire being is moved, sometimes literally. I say 'yes' over and over again and catch myself only at the end, wondering what I have just agreed to."

*Often after receiving Eucharist, I quietly pray in tongues, a gift that is hard to explain but utterly filling and beautiful for me. Human words disappear and my soul converses with God so fluently.

- **Who are the people in your life that you wish could know God?**

- **How can you pray for them to see Christ in you?**

- **What types of prayer time most deeply fill your soul so total peace can be felt? How often do you make sure you have space and time to be in full union with God?**

Life-Song Seeker

Seek Me this year,
not in the grandiose ways of largesse living
but through dignified moments of the heart speaking its truth.
To each soul a song has been placed, waiting to be heard,
for the songs of life provide a beauty only heaven can marvel at.

Soundless in brilliance, the life song of hearts
beating in tune within My heart, offer intimate praise,
brush the strokes of love from My choices of unknown wisdom.

Trust the guidance that slivers in and out of veins,
taps knowledge into the brain to procure movement,
and challenges the status quo;
or surrender to a massive Love -
instruction to create beauty.

Be a seeker, but first look within.
Hold your life as an offering of joy,
then surrender the way to My own.
Wings of inspiration surround you,
heal you, and carry you back home.

As you lay your life as gift,
freed from all willful inhibitions,
we sing in harmony as I teach.
Attune your soul to the direction of beaming hearts
awaiting the grace and love only you bring –
Me through your heart, your eyes, your hands or smile – to them.

Captivated by My voice you can be
seeker
giver and
light haven
for all
to restore their shine,
strengthen their voice,
proclaim their own prostration
of tear-stained praise.

January 5, 2014
Feast of the Epiphany

Personal Focus

After 4 pages of talking to God in my journal, my voice ended with this prayer. *"Captivated by a calling of my own but not wholly my own, I tread steps, make imprints, and wonder of their marks. I am captivated by grace, Yours in my life, and the beauty of how You shine through others. A life task, to tug upon sparks and turn them into flames, most vividly to fan flames already lit to shine in steadfast brilliance."* God picked up from there and answered all that I couldn't even capture in human words.

- *Be a seeker, but first look within.* **What are you seeking from God today, this month, for your life this year?**

- **What, or where in your life, do you need to allow God's song to internally "massage" out the stress and doubt?**

- *Lay your life as gift, freed from all willful inhibitions.* **Name your talents/gifts, including things you don't let others see. Looking at your list, how do you use them to serve God? Or, what prevents you from sharing these God-given talents?**

Chapter 8
Plunging into Mercy

Your path in life, the things that come your way
and rock your world, also affects your prayer.

As you change, prayer changes
in how you show-up, relate, and choose to hear God.

In difficult times, you can choose
to grow deeper and step back.

Enter these messages with your own questions,
concerns, doubts, and need to hear how God
might respond to your own rocky path.

Give your all to God and He plunges you
into His beautiful Divine Mercy.

Instructions of Grace

Rocked in the core of your essence,
you come into this world
to be made whole in giftedness,
to reach out into branches of light,
to seep into places unseen yet ready to receive.

When you are aware,
the task is both easier in knowing, yet taxing,
as the call is greater to be in integrity to your soul's calling.

Listen and trust the nature of simple truths shared in your path.
With eyes to see, accept the truth of love given.
My Presence permeates all aspects of life,
if you choose to see, feel, and know the essence of
purified peace in the small folds of light throughout the world.

Be amongst the messengers who can receive all of Me,
gift this to others, and seek to be refined in My love.
You know. Do not doubt.
Yes, child – hold onto My love,
the instructions of grace dancing upon your cells,
this makes you!

The vibrancy you possess then radiates;
comes because you are meant to teach in your life.
Though singular in one context, you are far from being alone –
the possibility for that pairing still exists.
Simply walk as you do.

June 13, 2013

Personal Focus

On this day I wrote about being blessed to go back to a town where I loved working, formerly as a High School Youth Minister. After 5 years, my role there ended due to a change of leadership getting rid of my role. This prayer entry came 2 years after leaving but coming back to support some of my former teens and feel in awe to see them now as young adults. At this special college concert, I heard a sentence from a parent that tugged at my heart. My leaving from the parish was done quietly (their call, not mine.) This parent saw me and shared: "You disappeared. I went to church because of you and since you aren't there, neither am I...." She helped me see what I sensed but hadn't named. My role is never just for the youth. It's also for the adults. As I was currently looking yet again for a new job, prayer was an action of watching, listening, and wondering.

- **What, do you sense, are your life instructions from God? How are you supposed to offer His grace in the world?**

- **Similarly, what doubts do you have about your calling – about who you are as a person of faith?**

Cultivating God's Breath

Giver of Breath, that is what I seem to need now: breath, new life, new understanding. In this week which was truly not a happy one and full of continued stress, I have tried to remind myself to breathe into Your presence. You remain constant. I remain ever faltering in my ability to follow through. I have not changed the essence of how I work, even though I am conscious and try to be quiet, to not stir up trouble – all this, as I re-read the prayer and conversations written. You are clear in me being bold – a catalyst, a person who inspires or begins the change. Will I survive? Better yet, can I thrive in an environment that operates so opposite of me in both logic and in heart? Can an unspoken prayer be answered in another's quietness? … My prayer is to find the shelter, a stronger barricade of support, so I trust that me "fighting" is worth it. Help me!

You touched My heart, held Me tight.
The precision of your knowledge
and desire of the ever-flowing pool of mercy
still exists in you - not as a theory, but as a memory.

In living so deeply,
the stance of desire to serve others has continually been shaken
[yet] what remains is solid strength and childlike trust.

Innocence glides under the radar
as expectations of human growth pull over the reality of ways.
The cloth does not fit a soul clinging to Me.
You have never changed from this steadfast place.

What captures you is only love and joy, leading you back into Me.
The breath of life sought contains the living cells of My existence.

Taste this in trueness and all else pales.
Scripture dances in your veins – you know this.
So why be surprised when what you do,
who you are, is unwelcomed among friends?
The message you bring of faith is not easily heard –
living being of Spirit rather than living "doer of action."

Your roundedness has to remain.

My words have to be absorbed.

Sit with the truth
of all you still are called to be.
You are known and know Me.
Continue to cultivate this precious trust.

June 28, 2014

Personal Focus

- *Twice in the message, God spoke of trust: childlike trust and precious trust.* What does trust mean to you? Do you have childlike trust in God? If not, can that be changed?

- *Living 'being of Spirit' or living 'doer of action'* Which category do you fit into? Do you struggle thinking one is 'better' than the other? Or, can you find a way for a healthy balance between the two?

- How often do you call upon the Holy Spirit to infuse into you all that is needed, even if that means stillness over action, or vice versa?

- Are you grounded in your relationship with the Trinity - God the Father, God the Son, God the Holy Spirit? If you feel work needs to be done, what steps can you take to change this?

Evidence of Breath

Present in circumstances beyond your control
you are invited to come
sit in the chaos
and observe the nuances of patterns
which formed this time and place for the unraveling to begin.
There is still wisdom in quietness, depth in shallow changes.

If your heart hears and trusts the opportunity for goodness,
then goodness shall flow.
Tidal waves are evidence easily captured;
breaths are still monumental –
inspire, exhale - lifeforce of inner wealth –
soul oxygen is still present.

For some, the dirt of living service, hand upon wood,
is My only opening in;
the container of understanding still needs to grow.
Re-envision yourself and your role.
While your spirit is tired, you can still thrive.
You have now named what you miss -
in letting go, more can come.

Your strength is focus and intensity;
allow for freedom in your serenity.
I do not fail
nor do I forget.
As your heart still seeks, it too is open.
May it be so.

~Your Loving God~
July 28, 2014

Personal Focus

God of silence & stillness, coming back to a non-rushed day should have been easy for me and yet, I woke up without a voice and needed a strong acupuncture treatment to help my back. My body is struggling, per usual, as I try to understand my placement in life once again. I want to share the natural and easy way of being connected to You. You have to provide clear avenues, inspiration and people. Today's Gospel is of the mustard seed. Is my faith strong enough to be a mustard seed of faith in my new workplace?

- **When you feel like you are "sitting in chaos," how do you navigate the steps for the future?**

- **What is your strength in life, in faith, that allows your heart and spirit to continue moving when you are exhausted?**

- **What stops you from slowing down? Do you believe that "doing nothing" isn't acceptable to God?**

Divine Mercy Sunday

After a very LONG entry of my writing to God, the time ended with this aspect of a more prayerful tone to God and then God's message to me.

My God show me Your Divine Mercy in my walk in life. Gently and swiftly lift me now from one place and easily into the next. I will not waiver in the prayer of my heart from January to about April 28th – don't know how or why, but may it be so in joy…

Today!? Mass – moments of beautiful strength and unspoken messages. I wanted depth today and hoped for a SMMP Mass but needed sleep and to be at SR for the Chapel time, too. Communion: the warmth and absolute comfort given in St. Raphael's arms was a tremendous gift. My tears acknowledged what my eyes could not say. I felt two angels and then I felt folded into one of them. If only that absolute peace and trust could remain in "body memory." We spoke. You gifted me in new 'protection' and again there were tears of acknowledgement, of knowing. I could not have the usual Spirit conversation due to the lack of singing but wanted to be immersed in that aspect of prayer.

You have invited me so richly into Your heart of mercy; the rays of light You shine warm my being, protect, and enrich my life. The prayer from the novena on Thursday so interestingly spoke to my life; not comprehending how or why, just knowing that I am to walk, to love, and to serve. That, because of Your love in me, Your love will be received by those able to see and experience Your love through another.

I praise You for coming through me - even on days like recently – when I felt so utterly depleted and unworthy due to what feels like doubt or mistrust. I doubt me and my ability to survive on my own. I know I am not getting thru any of this without You. I walk, give, and minister because of you. Why You have chosen me to serve after [such painful] experiences is not understood.

The sins of the powerful so profoundly affect the ones beneath them. You, in Your Divine Mercy apparently choose to constantly raise me up. I feel foolish in the eyes of the world and yet utterly sound in You. I do not see You – but I know You, Your voice, Your love. I cannot pretend to not believe or act differently. Strengthen me to know my place in serving and rest in assurance of Your love to care for my needs and desire too – to play a bit with family and friends. I do not want to always be alone!

God to Me
Reaching into the abyss of warm safety,
a place of profound joy is given and juxtaposed
with the pain felt from how you arrive.
Mercy and sacrifice require love not always understood.

To see into My eyes and hear the truth
opens your soul into streams of mercy
abounding through your being.
As you desire intimacy to be shared,
this is My heart calling you home closer to be fed and held.
Happiness gifted will cleanse the pain
coursing in emotions untamed.

The curtain of My fold of mercy
opens to all who desire to live in acknowledgement
of love given a name and sacrifice a price –
lives lifted up and into Me come out uniquely changed.

For your yes, I shower you with gifts of praise
which only your heart can recognize,
the child-like faith, naming moments of sweetness,
holding My hand in the world.

Tendrils of clouds formed in the sky have shown My love,
with eyes to see the message is clear:
the heart in the sky, the angel to guide and protect homes in life.
Remain in mystery of all that has a clear answer
yet delights the soul,
My handiness then sparkles in unexpected rays.

Be doused in the healing light
of crystal-like water dazzling in the sunlight.

Be prepared in the strength of mercy
covering your soul to then be and give to others.

Home in the folds of My heart, I keep you nourished.

Come often.

Reminders of Divine life will continue
to feed you as the path continues.

You remain in Me,
loved deeply
and walk willingly as servant and friend in My name.

April 7, 2013

Personal Focus

Reflect on your relationship with God.

- Are you bold and daring enough to risk opening the curtain to feel His love more deeply? If instead you feel hesitant, what stops you?

- At times, what might hold you back from "showing up to God and sharing your pain and scars" so they can be transformed?

- Can you name, and choose to seek healing, for past (or current) events in life that plague your soul from fully trusting Jesus?

Fire & Ocean of Mercy

Faithful God of fellowship – I have found You in living Word, through some people this week and I am grateful for those blessings. Intensity overflows it seems and I am conscious of all which both got me here and is getting me through! ... *(lots of sharing of events)* All around me in the struggle, when I seek and need it, goodness surrounds me.

I have covered you child, rest easy in My love.
The turmoil of this time prepares you in strength
to move beyond what is known
to live a reality which remains imbedded in faith
to be seen and felt in a myriad of ways,
* none of which can be ritualized into rote actions.*

Flames cannot consume a fluid vessel of love,
for what you desire to be remains, still,
an instrument of My voice – my nudging in your life.

The prophet's call does remain. You cannot turn away.
In quietly standing bright and boldly speaking,
'you cause unrest where complacency grew,' that is who you are.
Some will be able to handle the effects of your soul; others will not.

You remain open to continue trying to turn on lights,
* ignite passion in others.*

The calm living within you does not run dry.
The ocean of mercy will cleanse your being with profound joy.
It is coming child, and as you bless others along your way,
the path gets brighter, too.

I bring together people for reason not always seen,
but your hearts rejoice in being found in family not of this world.
Remain unafraid.
I will tend the fires,
strengthen the center of your lives,
and allow you to keep giving to others.
See with My grace,
it is here that My love then sparkles
and covers the earth in ways unimaginable.

Be held child. I have the rest.
Beloved Creator

April 13, 2013

Personal Focus

- Yet again, what is your calling in life? How are you choosing to shine bright with God's love? Or, is something still holding you back in fear?

- Do you know yourself, your inhibitions, and fears, well enough to name and give them to God? If so, make a practice to name what plagues you and invite God into what feels messy.

- *We all have events/people/feelings that cause pain like a 3rd degree emotional and spiritual burn. Tending to the pain allows new skin to grow to uncover our true calling, to be a vessel of love.* **How do you tend to any pain in your life?**

- How are you allowing your life to be "an instrument of God's voice?"

Vineyard of Heart

The simplest heartbeat can beat in time to its Maker.
It knows where it belongs,
holds fast to mercy of life entrusted at life's breath
danced upon the soul.

Remembering comes gently at times
and fights a deep breeze of uncertain fear of others.
May the remembering of love be all you need
to step one moment to the next,
on a path uncharted and yet safely guarded
in the manner gifted and chosen for your soul.

Beam the presence of Spirit
soaking into cracks of concrete life –
just because you cannot see does not mean purpose lacks.

Working in the vineyard of My heart
asks only that you love Me
and serve what is nobly known and in-scripted into cells,
woven wondrously in your heart.

Be in union with Me,
in quiet, in peace, in sickness, and in health.
My Presence does not change.
I am partnered to your soul.
Listen. Your soul speaks so clearly to Me,
I feed it in ways proper to its purpose.
Believe always in goodness. Shower the blessings.
And trust you are still held.

October 5, 2014
Feast of St. Faustina

Personal Focus

I showed up to prayer surprised (yet shouldn't be) that I was feeling fine the prior day/night with a friend and at Mass yet woke up rather sick. My physical being is affected by many known and unknown factors, including being with others and wanting to help them. Before the longer entry above, I ended my sharing with: *I need You Jesus to live, breathe, understand & serve. I desire still to love, offer, minister, and care. I feel changes in friends' comings and goings and yet my heart still holds love in loss.*

Scripture states the harvest is plenty, but laborers are few. **Evaluate yourself in terms of a "worker for God."**

- **What are your strengths?**

- **What are your weaknesses?**

- **What is your effort level in spending time with God to know His will *for* the work called of your soul?**

Unspoken Strength

The world awaits you child, so dear. There is a formidable strength to your spirit which has [been tested] and cannot ever be broken. As you belong to Me, reside in My heart, desire to do My will, I am aware of your struggles, pains, and desires. You are not incapable of succeeding where you are; in fact, you have succeeded, but different paths always offer more opportunities for light and growth.

Remain in touch with the life blood of Spirit running through your veins and do not confuse your stubborn will for My will. Test yourself to know where you stand and why. You are clear on issues and sometimes your resolve for truth cannot be accepted - you must rest in Spirit while not liking how, or why.

The feast you long for comes brilliantly in moments of utter praise when you are free to express the glory wound into you. Just because you cannot freely praise and cannot engage deeply in prayer due to surroundings and circumstances, this does not mean I cannot find and fill you quietly, differently.

Intimacy of shared experiences of radiant visions are unmatched at times. Who you are and what you hold is meant to grace many, but not always in ways you expect or even understand in worldly ways. You call to you those who can grow from the gift of your living in Me. Yes, similarly others remain at a distance and cannot express what you most love.

The teaching of spirituality remains present in life walks and choices of will. This has been a huge part of your lesson [at job then] – owning a beauty of you and realizing all cannot – or rather do not desire – to climb into My lap.

You struggle because you are a child, want to play and see the world as the joy it can be, looking beyond what is now. Do not fear – you can, do, and will continue to succeed. Let go. Continue to trust – to sit with Me. Your communication is a constant opening into My depths, even though your humanity pulls you away at times.

You always desire Me – and child, yes – you do also always deserve Me at your side. As you hide from your Gramma not wanting to share your pain, you cannot hide from Me – even when words are not in ink, we still converse deeply. Don't you know how deeply woven you also remain in Me?

As you desire a physical expression of inner need – cuddling into strength of one who loves you, seek to cuddle into My Spirit's embrace so that you remember, always, who you are. Your journey is not one which makes sense to you –cannot as it is wrought with pain and a calling to remain when others walk away?

You call forth a witness to Me in your actions – your peace residing in Me, which is the truth you know, the truth you fight for. Speak your piece to be heard. Do not battle. Walk solely into My arms, I do not leave you.

The forced motions of prayer grate your spirit. The submitting of your will and spiritual path to another [person] feels like a desecration to your walk in this life. For the time being, do what brings outer peace as inner peace will come later. Dance with desires remaining in your heart. All you seek is not forgotten: the right place, the right time. You are called, chosen, loved, and surrounded, even when you feel so completely lost.

[The following is still how I heard God speaking to me, however the message is not italicized to allow it to stand out.]

I am woven into moments of unique
and unspeakable prayer.
I am guarded deeply by souls
who commit to an unspoken task
to surrender to My voice, a calling known but not heard.

In the whispers of unspoken praise
the Presence I am softens the places bound in fear.
The world does not change on its own,
only through individuals who see beyond
and into the veil of My flesh where beauty resides
and flows in abundance onto and into thirsting souls.

Though I am for all, not all come.
Though some seek, they do so only until their limits
[are met], unwillingly to move beyond.

Remain in the cloister of My all protecting heart
holding you profoundly in the center of all you are,
all you need to be.

As long as you walk with and into Me,
the world's answers shall not matter,
cannot affect your call –
your soul purpose to gently teach and strongly love.

Listen at levels of radiant love
sparkling as a new stream flowing through you.

Be wrapped in My mercy, found in My embrace.
As you seek this home, your only true home,
you can return to yourself and your worldly home
with immeasurable gifts which will guide you
to places and situations to live your call –
as long as you are able, and they choose to see.

Be both servant to Me
and leader to others in your gentle strength.
You teach without words and counsel with a wisdom
grown in life witness to My Name.

Remain in Me.
Lean into Me.
Open your hands, always, to receive
the treasures which change as the times grow weary.

Your presence is crafted, known, and loved.
Honor all this, which is you,
so to bring this fruit to others.

In love,
Your Creator, Life-Sustaining, Loving God

February 1, 2013

Personal Focus

The entire entry was God speaking so clearly to my needs.

As this volume of prayer entries ends, I cannot come up with questions for you. This specific entry feeds and reminds me of my purpose and offers strength. I encourage you to bring your deepest need, fears, doubts, and concerns to mind and then read this entry again (and maybe repeatedly, I do!) See how God speaks directly to you from this prayer.

- **What do you need to hear from God?**

- **What do you need to speak to God?**

- **How open are you to receiving God's voice?**

"Encounter" – closing thoughts

As a lover of the Word and of words, I also admire the beauty that comes from traditional artists using color, form, shades, and lighting to evoke emotion from images born in their soul and transferred to canvas. For that reason, there was no doubt about the artist's work I hoped to have on the cover. For at least two decades Mary Southard's artwork has spoken to me and what I have heard matches what I write in prayer. But choosing the cover for this book was not cut and dry. I sought advice from friends looking at a few options Mary recommended, and I even asked for more options only to ironically land back at my first choice. I wanted the image to capture the essence of this first book. It took time, and trusting inner guidance, to listen to the image. In doing so I understood why Mary recommended, and I couldn't back away from, "Encounter" the female version of Moses and the burning bush.

I love sharing with youth that after the fall, Moses was the only person in the Bible who spoke with God face to face. What a gift! Yet, those wandering in the desert with Moses became deeply afraid *of God seeing them* and eventually seeing God face to face ceased to happen. If you were offered intimacy through an encounter with our one true God, how would you feel surrounded by this immensity of Love and pure Light?

Would you be afraid? Would you want to soak in the experience of awe? Or be embraced by it, holding it close and capturing it so you too can share it? That is what this image of "Encounter" speaks to me and why I chose it: depth of an intimate, loving relationship and the transforming qualities this relationship with God offers to each seeker. There is tremendous peace being surrounded in the beautiful depth of Love and in allowing our relationship with God the Father, Jesus our Savior, and the Holy Spirit our Advocate – all in One – to alter, or better yet lead, our path in life.

If you followed the roadmap of prayers offered in this book, you have graduated from hesitantly seeking a relationship with God to feeling His stillness and peace in prayer. You have tiptoed into what it looks like to be held in God's glorious heart and how His strength *gives you strength.* You have explored God's personal canvas with his magnificent palette of colors and treasures waiting to be discovered and appreciated in nature. In seeing God's hand and creativity everywhere, His love infuses into your soul and teaches it to surrender to His endearing peace.

Thus, fully embraced in this love the next few steps are not so daunting! It is a daily choice to continually lean into trust. The prayer of Divine Mercy is "Jesus, I trust in You" and while that should be easy, our humanity gets in the way. Yet living with the choice to trust, it is possible to move through, and even live in difficulties, and then choose to gift praise, to sing thanksgiving amid the joys and pains of life.

Because we are here hoping for "on earth as it is in heaven," God's mercy is needed for our own path, for those in our path, and most certainly the world. Encountering God, stepping into our own intimate relationship with Jesus, allowing the Holy Spirit to overtake our GPS, we are led deeper into the gaze of Christ, amplifying our soul's created longing to one day be back and encounter our Creator face to face.

I sincerely hope these prayers helped your inner GPS to surrender more to Jesus' love, to see things differently, and desire to spend time with Jesus in your heart each day. The only way I know how to survive is by living in, with and through the One who loves me the most – God-Jesus-Holy Spirit – three in One. May you continue to dance with the Spirit and remain rooted in Light.

"SO, AS YOU RECEIVED CHRIST JESUS THE LORD, **WALK** IN HIM, **ROOTED** IN HIM AND BUILT UPON HIM AND **ESTABLISHED** IN THE FAITH AS YOU WERE TAUGHT, ABOUNDING IN **THANKSGIVING.**"
COLOSSIANS 2:6-7

ACKNOWLEDGEMENTS

Mom *(Mary Sue Krakora)* – Ever my chief editor, in Jr. High I sought the wisdom of your eyes and mind to help with my papers and grew under your tutelage. I still seek your approval and need help to fine tune content. Your help in editing the introduction and closing thoughts is fitting for your role – the person who first taught me faith and provided the foundation to know and love God. And the closing thoughts? I know you are my greatest supporter **(dad too!)** and provider of protection and healing through prayer. Your faith, witness, and prayers pave the way for my eternal home.

Mary Southard, CSJ *(Artist)* **& Debra Hanrahan** *(assistant to Mary)* – The immediate response of a "yes" I could use a piece of art made my soul smile! I appreciated your willingness to read prayers and choose art that you felt matched words. Most especially I appreciated the *patience* with my emails in the drawn-out choosing process. Thank you, Mary, for sharing your gift with the world! Your art is my visual prayer of strength, depth, and joy!

Heidi Shelter Oliver – Your practical spirituality and generous heart took me in 15 years ago for nine months and offered protection with a physical roof and an understanding heart. In that time, I nurtured new roots and unknowingly found space to secure my Catholic faith in a time of uncertainty. Your family and friends gave me space to seek, cry, and dance. Thank you for a special friendship and sharing your eyes, literal in editing for the first round, and spiritual in understanding me and what I hoped to say!

Lucy Griffin –You moved seamlessly from an irreplaceable assistant & catechist to a dear friend. Every faith-filled conversation we had nourished my soul in the giving and *(as you shared)* your soul in the receiving. Knowing my prayer writings fed your soul swung wide the door to begin this long encouraged first book. Thank you for the "how to read Julie," being top in my list of advice seekers and idea sharers for faith, how to compile this book, and much more!

West DuPage Deanery 2018-2020 Colleagues – Collaboration and community are necessary to survive in ministry. In serving as co-chair of our great group, the Holy Spirit opened a door for me. You all allowed me to offer and unknowingly (to me) test pilot ideas for this book. Each time I shared a prayer with you and had us reflect your positive feedback affirmed it was time.

Diane Ahlemeyer – "I am you; you are me…" you helped comically sing our way through difficult courses in grad school and our paths crossed again to become colleagues. Your task was on a larger scope to offer feedback to make this the best offering of prayers to help other adult seekers on their journey. As you were honored when I asked and humbled to read, I am equally blessed and humbled to know that my relationship with Jesus has helped you.

Dear Prayerful Seekers,

As an author of my first book of personal prayers, I am honored that you chose to buy this book; or, if gifted with it chose to read it! **Thank you for choosing to take time for yourself and invite God deeper into your soul.** I would truly love to hear from you and especially how any of these prayers have assisted you in your prayer life and relationship with our Triune God.

Message me at:
inkandvessel@gmail.com

Facebook Group: **Ink & Vessel**